A Short Treatise on the Metaphysics of Tsunamis

Studies in Violence, Mimesis, and Culture

A Short Treatise on the Metaphysics of Tsunamis

Jean-Pierre Dupuy

Translated by M. B. DeBevoise

Michigan State University Press · *East Lansing*

♾ The paper used in this publication meets the minimum requirements of ANSI/NISO
Z39.48-1992 (R 1997) (Permanence of Paper).

 Michigan State University Press
East Lansing, Michigan 48823-5245

Printed and bound in the United States of America.

21 20 19 18 17 16 15   1 2 3 4 5 6 7 8 9 10

LIBRARY OF CONGRESS CONTROL NUMBER: 2015936766
ISBN: 978-1-61186-185-3 (pbk.)
ISBN: 978-1-60917-472-9 (ebook: PDF)
ISBN: 978-1-62895-244-5 (ebook: ePub)
ISBN: 978-1-62896-244-4 (ebook: Kindle)

Book design by Charlie Sharp, Sharp Des!gns, Lansing, Michigan
Cover design by David Drummond, Salamander Design, www.salamanderhill.com
The Great Wave at Kanagawa, ca. 1830–32, by Katsushika Hokusai, 1760–1849, © The
Metropolitan Museum of Art. Used courtesy of the Metropolitan Museum of Art, H. O.
Havemeyer Collection, Bequest of Mrs. H. O. Havemeyer, 1929 (JP1847).

g green press Michigan State University Press is a member of the Green Press
INITIATIVE Initiative and is committed to developing and encouraging ecologically
responsible publishing practices. For more information about the Green Press Initiative
and the use of recycled paper in book publishing, please visit *www.greenpressinitiative.org*.

Visit Michigan State University Press at *www.msupress.org*

Contents

A Note on the Translation

A decade has now passed since this book first appeared in France, in 2005. The original edition has been brought over into English with only a small number of changes. In the third chapter the text has been slightly altered by the author, and a long note added, to take into account recent scholarship concerning the controversy over Hannah Arendt's reading of the Eichmann case. Minor errors of fact or emphasis have been silently corrected elsewhere.

In a few places the author has removed a very brief passage that seems, in retrospect, to detract from the force of the argument, or that, irrelevantly from the point of view of American readers, takes issue with the usual French translation of a particular term. For the opposite reason I have added a number of notes on my own account, in order to clarify points of detail that may be of interest to the same readers.

The appendix is new, containing a brief essay on the Fukushima disaster that was published as an op-ed piece in *Le Monde* in March 2011, under the title "Une catastrophe monstre," and now appears for the first time in English.

Acknowledgments

In the interval between giving the lecture that forms the basis for this book and its publication, I have benefited from the comments of many colleagues and friends, among them Monique Canto-Sperber, Thierry Gaudin, Gérard Toulouse, Henri Renon, Lucien Scubla, Alexei Grinbaum, Anne-Marie Mercier-Faivre, Chantal Thomas, Philippe Colomb, Michel Chaduteau, Simon Charbonneau, Gérard Malkassian, Pierre Léna, Fabrice Flipo, Georges-Yves Kervern, Paul-Henri Bourrelier, Gilbert Filleul, Daniel Ramirez, Bertrand Munier, Laurent LeGuyader, and Claude Habib.

To all of them, my warmest thanks. And especially to Richard Figuier for introducing me to the work of Günther Anders.

CHAPTER 1

Genesis

Only a god can save us now.
—Martin Heidegger

Now, at last, it has become plain that the same proud spirit of humanism that gives our world its astonishing and unprecedented dynamism also imperils the future of human society itself. We are living today in the shadow cast by the prospect of catastrophes that, separately or in combination, threaten to bring about the disappearance of the human race from the earth. Our responsibility is all the more enormous as we become more and more convinced that we are the sole cause of what will happen to us. And yet there is a danger that our sense of our own responsibility will increase, rather than diminish, the very arrogance that gave rise to it. Once we have persuaded ourselves that the salvation of the world is in our hands, that humanity owes it to itself to be its own savior, there is a risk we will rush headlong into the abyss. With every passing day, this panicked flight comes nearer to being the destiny of mankind.

Mourning for the Future

The German Jewish philosopher Günther Anders (1902–1992) was the most profound and the most daring of the many thinkers who contemplated the great catastrophes of the twentieth century. He is less well known than two of his classmates at Marburg, like him students of Heidegger: his future wife Hannah Arendt and his friend Hans Jonas. Anders's relative obscurity is a consequence not only of his own stubbornness, but also of the fragmented character of his writings. He abjured great systematic treatises in favor of topical investigations, and not infrequently resorted to parable. More than once, for example, he recounted the biblical tale of the flood in a distinctive and original way. Noah, in his telling, had grown tired of being a prophet of doom whom no one any longer took seriously, for he was forever announcing a catastrophe that never came. And so one day he clothed himself in sackcloth and covered his head with ashes:

> Only a man who was mourning [the death of] a beloved child or his wife was allowed to do this. Clothed in the garb of truth, bearer of sorrow, he went back to the city, resolved to turn the curiosity, spitefulness, and superstition of its inhabitants to his advantage. Soon a small crowd of curious people had gathered around him. They asked him questions. They asked if someone had died, and who the dead person was. Noah replied to them that many had died, and then, to the great amusement of his listeners, said that they themselves were the dead of whom he spoke. When he was asked when this catastrophe had taken place, he replied to them: "Tomorrow." Profiting from their attention and confusion, Noah drew himself up to his full height and said these words: "The day after tomorrow, the flood will be something that will have been. And when the flood will have been, *everything that is will never have existed.* When the flood will have carried off everything that is, everything that will have been, it will be too late to remember, for there will no longer be anyone alive. And so there will no longer be any difference between the dead and those who mourn them. *If I have come before you, it is in order to reverse time*, to mourn tomorrow's dead today. The day after tomorrow it will be too late." With this he went back whence he had come, took off the sackcloth [that he wore], cleaned his face of the ashes that covered it, and went to his workshop. That evening

a carpenter knocked on his door and said to him: "Let me help you build an ark, *so that it may become false.*" Later a roofer joined them, saying: "It is raining over the mountains, let me help you, *so that it may become false.*"[1]

The tragedy that awaits anyone who dares to prophesy catastrophe is beautifully condensed in this magnificent parable, which nevertheless indicates to us the way out from an apparently paralyzing impasse.

The prophet of doom is not heard because his words, even if they issue from secure knowledge and true information, do not manage to penetrate the system of beliefs held by those to whom they are addressed. It is not enough to know in order to accept what one knows and then to act on it. This fundamental reality is foreign to the so-called precautionary principle, whose implicit premise is that we do not act in the face of catastrophe because we are not sure of knowing enough to act effectively.[2] It is plain, however, that even when we know something with certainty, we may be incapable of believing what we know. The existence and dramatic consequences of global warming were known, and made known to the world, more than a quarter-century ago. But scientists were crying out in the wilderness. It is true that their predictions suffer from one great imprecision: nobody can exactly locate the average rise in global temperature, by the end of the twenty-first century, within a broad range of between two and six degrees Celsius (or about four and eleven degrees Fahrenheit).[3] And yet it seems not to be generally understood that half of this uncertainty is the result of uncertainty about the type of action that will be taken to reduce greenhouse-gas emissions. Is it really because we do not know how we would react to a forecast of impending doom that we do not act? The suggestion is absurd. Moreover, there is this one thing of which we are quite certain: if China, India, and Brazil go on pursuing the course of development that we have given them as a model to be imitated, we will enter into a looking-glass world in which surprises (not only regarding the climate, but many other things as well) will be routine, the exception will be the rule, and our capacity to act in and on the world will have become a power of destruction.

Searching for the reason why many European Jews refused until the very end, even on the railway platform at Auschwitz-Birkenau, to believe in the reality of industrial extermination, Primo Levi quoted an old German adage: "Things whose existence is not morally possible cannot exist." Our ability not to see when faced with the obviousness of suffering and atrocities is the principal obstacle that the prophet of doom must at least find a way around, if he cannot actually overcome it.

The precautionary principle is ritually invoked not only in support of the view that more must be known, and therefore more research carried out, before we can act; it is also accompanied by an appeal to our sense of ethical obligation. But ethics, if it is to be of any help to us, must prompt us to call into question an idea that is so commonly accepted it has already become a cliché, namely, that we are obliged to answer to future generations for our actions.

The recourse to the language of rights, duties, and responsibility in examining our moral relationship to future generations presents conceptual difficulties that Western philosophy has, for the most part, proved incapable of clearing up. A recent and eloquent example of this failure may be found in John Rawls's magnum opus, *A Theory of Justice*, imagined by its author and his admirers to have both summed up and superseded all previous works of modern moral and political philosophy. Having rigorously stated and established, at least to his own satisfaction, the principles of justice that must order the basic institutions of a democratic society, Rawls nevertheless cannot avoid concluding that these principles do not apply to questions of intergenerational fairness. He is aware that this is a serious problem, but the remedy he proposes is vague and, at best, no more than provisional.

The source of Rawls's difficulty is the irreversibility of time. A theory of justice based on contractual obligation embodies, by definition, the ideal of reciprocity. But there can be no reciprocity between generations, at least not after some rather brief interval, for whereas later generations inherit the works of those who have gone before, they are unable to give anything in return. But the trouble goes deeper than this. In the Western perspective of linear time, itself inseparable from eighteenth-century ideas of progress, it is assumed that future generations will be happier and wiser than previous generations. But Rawls's theory of justice, precisely because it formalizes a fundamental moral intuition, that priority should be given to the most dis-advantaged members of society, leads to the paradox that the first in a line of generations is the worst off and yet its members are the only ones able to confer benefits on those who come after them.[4] Kant, who had already detected the problem in *Idea for a Universal History from a Cosmopolitan Point of View* (1784), found it inconceivable (*rätselhaft*) that the course of human history could be imagined to resemble the construction of a home that only the last generation would have the privilege of inhabiting. And yet he was unable to free himself from the spell cast by a ruse of nature, or perhaps of history, by which prior generations are led to sacrifice themselves for later generations—the height of the very same instrumental conception of practical reason he rejected.

Our situation today is very different, for our main concern is how to avoid global catastrophe. Is this to say that we must substitute for the idea of human advancement one of decay and decline? Stating the matter in this way, as a choice between progress and decadence, is quite pointless. We can say altogether opposite things about the age in which we live and they will be equally true (for example, that our age is both the most exhilarating and the most frightening of all). We must keep two things in mind at once, the possibility of catastrophe and the possibly cosmic responsibility that falls to humanity of trying to avert this catastrophe. At the table where the parties to Rawls's social contract sit, all generations are equal: the claims of no one generation have greater weight than those of others. But plainly generations are not equal from the moral point of view. Ours and the ones that will follow us have considerably greater moral knowledge, as it were, than previous generations, of whom it may be said today, by contrast with ourselves, that they did not know what they were doing. We are now witnessing the emergence of humanity as a quasi-subject, the dawning awareness that its destiny is self-destruction, and the birth of an absolute responsibility to avoid this self-destruction.

As for our own responsibility, it is not addressed to future generations—these anonymous beings whose existence is purely virtual, and in whose happiness and welfare it will never be possible to believe that we shall have any reason at all to take a genuinely personal interest. To cast our responsibility in terms of a requirement to achieve distributive justice across generations lands us in a dead end.[5]

It is in relation to the fate of humanity that our duty must be conceived, which is to say in relation to ourselves, here and now. Thus Dante, in the tenth canto of the *Inferno*:

So you understand how our awareness
will die completely at the moment when
the portal of the future has been shut.[6]

If the door to the future were to close, as a result of our own actions, the very meaning of human history would be forever destroyed, not only in prospect but in retrospect as well: "The day after tomorrow, the flood will be something that has been. And when the flood will have been, *everything that is will never have existed.*"

Can we find the conceptual resources we need by looking outside the Western tradition? Amerindian wisdom literature has bequeathed to us this very fine saying: "The earth is loaned to us by our children."[7] It expresses a cyclical conception of time that seems strange to our way of thinking. And yet the maxim takes on even greater force in a linear perspective, I believe, once the necessary mental adjustment has been made. Notwithstanding that our children—that is, the children of our children, and their children, and so on indefinitely—have neither physical nor legal existence, we are enjoined to reverse the flight of time's arrow and imagine that it is they who bring us the earth—which is to say everything that we value. We do not own nature, we have only the usufruct of it. From whom have we received it? From the future! Anyone who objects, "But the future is not real!" will have done nothing more than draw our attention to the stumbling block that confronts every philosophy of looming catastrophe: we fail to recognize, or do not recognize as we should, and as we must, the reality of the future.

Notice that the maxim is not content to reverse time; it reconfigures time into a loop. The maxim invites us to project ourselves into the future and to look back at the present from a point of view that we will ourselves have created, since we are the ones who make our children, biologically and, above all, morally. Through this act of imagination, by splitting time into two parts and then joining them together in the form of conscious experience, it may perhaps be possible to establish the reciprocity between present and future that is wanting. Whether or not the future has any need of us, we, for our part, need the future, for it is the future that gives meaning to everything that we do.

Noah's purpose in Anders's parable is to devise just such a reciprocity. In mourning the death of those who are still alive, he collapses the future into the past and so, in effect, negates time by transforming it into an eternal present. But the doomsayer's misfortunes have not yet come to an end. Either his prophecy proves to be true, and yet we show him no gratitude for having given us warning (if we do not actually accuse him of being the cause of the calamity he has rightly foreseen); or his forecast goes unfulfilled, the predicted catastrophe does not take place, and afterward he is mocked and ridiculed for having struck the pose of a Cassandra. But it was Cassandra's fate that her prophecies were never to be heeded. It seems not to have occurred to anyone that, if a catastrophe does not take place, it may be because warning was given beforehand and the warning was heeded. "The prophecy of doom is made to avert its coming," Hans Jonas observes, "and it would be the height of injustice later to deride the 'alarmists' because 'it did not turn out [to be] so bad after all.' To have been wrong may have been their merit."[8]

The paradox of doomsaying arises from the fact that the prospect of catastrophe can be made credible only if we can be persuaded first of its reality—of its existence as part of the future, which is itself a part of the ontological furniture of the world, in the jargon of analytic philosophers. In this conception, the predicted sufferings and deaths will inevitably occur; they are the unmistakable marks of an implacable destiny. The present preserves the memory of them, as it were, as a result of the mind's having projected itself into the time following the catastrophe, conceiving of the event in the future perfect tense: there exists a moment in the future that we may look forward to, and say of the prophesied catastrophe that at that moment it *will have* taken place; thus, for example, in Anders's parable, the flood is something that will have been, the day after tomorrow. If we succeed too well in doing this, however, we risk losing sight of our purpose, which is to heighten public awareness and bring about concerted action so that the catastrophe does not occur: "Let me help you build an ark, *so that it may become false.*"

The same paradox is at the heart of a classic figure of literature and philosophy, the killer judge, who "neutralizes" all those of whom it is written that they shall commit a crime—with the result that their crimes will not be committed.[9] Intuitively one feels that the paradox derives from the failure of the past prediction to be joined with the future event in a closed loop. But the very idea of such a loop makes no sense in our ordinary metaphysics, as the modal logic of prevention shows. Prevention consists in taking action to ensure that an unwanted action is relegated to the ontological realm of nonactualized possibilities. The catastrophe, even though it does not occur, retains the status of a possibility, not in the sense that it would still be possible for it to take place, but in the sense that it will forever remain true that it could have taken place. When one announces that a catastrophe is imminent, in order to avert it, this announcement does not possess the status of a prediction, in the strict sense of the term: one does not claim to say what the future will be, only what it would have been had preventive measures not been taken. There is no need for any loop to close here. The announced future does not have to coincide with the actual future, the forecast does not have to come true—for the announced "future" is not in fact the future at all, but a possible world that is, and will remain, nonactual.[10] The figure illustrated by the killer judge makes sense to us because it corresponds to what might be called common-sense metaphysics, in which time assumes the form of a branching tree within which the actual path of events can be traced. Time is a garden of forking paths, to quote Jorge Luis Borges, the most metaphysical of poets and the most poetic of metaphysicians.

The metaphysics implicit in Günther Anders's parable is obviously of another type. There time takes the form of a loop in which the past and the future reciprocally interact and determine each other. On this view, the future is no less fixed than the past: "When he was asked when this catastrophe had taken place, he replied to them: 'Tomorrow.' . . . The day after tomorrow, the flood will be something that has been"). One of the consequences of likening the future to destiny or fate is that any event that belongs neither to the past nor the future is impossible. From this it follows that precaution cannot take the form of prevention. Prevention supposes that an undesirable event, once prevented, is a nonactualized possibility; in other words, an event must be possible in order for us to have a reason to act to prevent it; but if our reaction is effective, the event does not occur. Such a state of affairs is impossible in the time-world of the prophet of doom.

The paradoxical character of catastrophe under the interpretation that I am urging should be no more disconcerting to the Western mind than the figure of the killer judge. The idea that a catastrophic event not only belongs to the future as something that is fated to happen, but at the same time is contingent and accidental, something that might not happen—even if, from the perspective of the future perfect, it appears to be necessary—is perfectly familiar to the man in the street, the common man, as he used to be called.

It is the metaphysical opinion of the meek, the ones who shall inherit the earth, according to the Gospel: they find it altogether natural to suppose that if a memorable event occurs, for example, the loss of a loved one, it was somehow bound to occur, while feeling at the same time that so long as it has not occurred, it is not inevitable. It is therefore the realization of the event— the fact that it actually occurs—that makes it retrospectively necessary.[11] Accordingly, the metaphysics that must serve as the basis for a precautionary doctrine adapted to an age of catastrophes requires us to project ourselves into the time that follows the dreaded event, and to see it in retrospect as an event that was both necessary and improbable. This is not, by the way, really a new idea: when Oedipus kills his father at the fatal crossroads near Delphi; when Meursault, Camus's "stranger," kills the Arab under the blazing sun in Algiers—these events appear to the Western mind as a matter of intuitive sensibility no less than philosophical tradition, as both accidents and inevitabilities in which chance and destiny coincide.[12] The metaphysics of doomsaying is the very same metaphysics that informs our understanding of tragedy, classical and modern alike.

Catastrophe and Evil

The reason I am in a position today to derive this abstract form from Günther Anders's parable is that I happened to isolate it independently of Anders and even before encountering his work. Several years ago I wrote a book sketching the outlines of a philosophical attitude, which I call enlightened doomsaying, aimed at helping us protect ourselves from ourselves.[13] It urges us, I pointed out by way of conclusion, "to regard the further existence of human society as the endlessly provisional result of negating an act of self-destruction—an act that is engraved in a future that has been frozen into fate."[14] I had begun by considering a series of historically recent threats to human civilization—climate change, the depletion of fossil resources and the energy crisis to which it has led, environmental degradation, novel strains of infectious disease, the frantic race to develop advanced technologies, and so on—and the policies proposed for dealing with them, which the precautionary principle is supposed to be qualified to adjudicate. The precautionary principle is quite incapable of doing anything of the sort, however, for in every case it was incontrovertibly clear that our knowledge of these threats, some of which are of the greatest seriousness, moves no one to action—and this because we do not believe what we know to be true, because we cannot bring ourselves to face up to the implications of what we know.

The manuscript of my book was all but complete by the end of August 2001, and I was about to send it to my publisher when the terrorist attacks of 11 September occurred. The next day I was astonished to hear a former CIA official say: "We knew, but we didn't believe what we knew." I decided at once to hold on to the manuscript and revise the discussion of catastrophe by taking into account all the ways in which humanity does its utmost to imperil its own survival, not only by destroying the very physical environment that permits societies to flourish, but also in perfecting unprecedented instruments of warfare that societies may use against one another. The risk of violence associated with nuclear deterrence, weapons of mass destruction, and terrorism now presented itself as an occasion and further justification for enlightened doomsaying.

In spite of its unavoidably speculative character, my book in its new form enjoyed a certain measure of success. It was bound to be speculative for a simple but profound reason. I hold, as Hans Jonas did, that any feasible answer to our problems can only be political in nature. But politics presupposes ethics, which in turn depends upon metaphysics. Nothing could be more plain than that none of the moral philosophies presently available to us is adequate to the predicament we face. Ethics must be given a new foundation so that it may be, in Jonas's phrase, an "ethics for the future," that is, a philosophy that makes preserving the future the foremost priority of mankind. The novel metaphysics that this ethics requires is the one I have just sketched in broad outline, in commenting on Anders's parable.

In arguing against the precautionary principle in my earlier book, I found myself in the awkward position of appearing to endorse the aims of groups and vested interests that took issue with the precautionary principle for reasons quite opposite to my own. The scientific and technological establishment, in particular, fiercely attacked the principle on the ground that it demanded an end to all research and innovation, to risk-taking of any kind. It will already be clear to readers of this book, I take it, that I make an altogether different argument. I hold that the precautionary principle, in failing to grasp the true nature of the threats we face, in laying emphasis on our ignorance when it is our inability, or unwillingness, to believe what we do know that is at issue, is supremely unsuited to helping us in our struggle for survival.

However much animosity and incomprehension the book aroused, it also brought a great deal of support and encouragement. The criticism that made the most lasting impression on me came from a Jewish intellectual: you speak of catastrophe in the future, he told me, but it has already taken place. He was thinking, of course, of Auschwitz. The most moving reassurance came from my own discovery of the work of Günther Anders. Until then this one of "Heidegger's children" had been entirely unknown to me. I had long been acquainted with the indispensable writings of Hannah Arendt, of course, and the notion of enlightened doomsaying is itself a consequence of my attempt to provide a basis for the imperative of responsibility (*das Prinzip Verantwortung*) and the ethics of the future elaborated by Hans Jonas, using the tools of analytical philosophy. Of the author of such works as *The Obsolescence of Mankind, We Sons of Eichmann*, and *Hiroshima Is Everywhere*, however, I knew nothing.[15] In these works I encountered a German Jewish thinker who did not hesitate to treat Hiroshima and Nagasaki as incomparable moral catastrophes. What is more, careful study of Anders's thought convinced me that he had already worked out the principles of enlightened doomsaying in considerable detail. The parable of Noah, for example, furnishes a splendid illustration of ideas that I had developed independently.

◆ ◆ ◆

It was not long before I had acquired the reputation of being, at best, a philosopher of catastrophe and, at worst, an irresponsible alarmist. My opinion on disasters of all sorts was regularly solicited. I knew that the year 2005 promised to bring a severe test of enlightened doomsaying with the commemoration of three great catastrophes, one natural, the other two moral, that profoundly influenced the modern history of the West, and particularly the way in which the problem of evil has come to be conceived: the 250th anniversary of the Lisbon earthquake (1 November 1755), and the sixtieth anniversary of both the discovery of the Auschwitz-Birkenau camp (27 January 1945) and the bombing of Hiroshima and Nagasaki (6 August and 9 August 1945, respectively).

I could hardly refuse, then, to accept an invitation from a group of eminent eighteenth-century historians at the University of Lyon to deliver the keynote address of a conference commemorating the Lisbon catastrophe and the upheaval it caused in Western thought.[16] I chose as my title "Lisbon, Auschwitz, Hiroshima, New York, Kyoto: A Philosophical Voyage in the Land of Catastrophe."

New York, in this title, symbolized more a date than a place: the eleventh day of September in the year 2001, when, with a slight delay, the twenty-first century made its horrifying debut. Kyoto, for its part, was meant to evoke the famous protocol adopted there several years earlier, although less for what the signatories ratified than for what they did not. Their proclamation warned of planetary disaster, but then nullified any sense of urgency by recommending the most halfhearted measures to prevent it—scarcely more than gestures, laughable for their timidity. To my way of thinking, Kyoto represents the catastrophe that is still to come.

In selecting these five catastrophes, from among many others, I was tacitly advancing a theoretical claim that I was well aware many would dispute. Two main arguments could be expected to be brought against me. First, if the scope of calamity, measured in numbers of victims, is the relevant criterion, then my list was shockingly skewed, since the death toll from the attacks on New York and Washington did not "even" reach the figure of three thousand. A philosopher was interviewed on this point:

> I've worked for a long time on violence; I attach importance to quantitative analysis. I noticed that the victims [of the 11 September attacks] are not more numerous than at Sabra and Shatila [in Lebanon] in 1982, and still fewer than during the Black September of 1970 in Jordan, where there were more than four thousand victims. . . . There are two indices for *measuring* violence: the victims, and possibly fear as well. Once again, on 11 September there were some three thousand civilians killed in a conflict that had not been declared. [It represented] a huge *symbolic* challenge to American supremacy, which inevitably produced collective fear, *but it was not a nuclear bomb.*[17]

Can anyone seriously dispute that is the degree zero, the nadir of thinking about evil? Numbers tell us nothing about evil. Whoever saves a life saves the world, according to the Talmud. One finds an echo of this view in the Gospels, in the parable reported by both Luke and Matthew: "What man of you, having a hundred sheep, if he loses one of them, does not leave the ninety-nine in the wilderness, and go after the one which is lost, until he finds it?"[18]

A much more serious objection was certain to be raised, however. I would be accused of lumping together catastrophes that have nothing to do with one another: natural catastrophes, on the one hand (Lisbon and Kyoto, though whether they can really be placed on the same level is far from obvious), and moral catastrophes (Auschwitz, Hiroshima, New York), on the other. In the eyes of my critics, this category error betrays a moral monstrosity. Here there was a choice with regard to the offense given: either I would be charged with treating the Shoah as a natural catastrophe, in which case the guilty are exonerated; or with comparing God to a gang of criminals. Since the latter error is considered today to be far less grave than the former, however, there could be little doubt that I would be accused of naturalizing evil.

But I knew what I was doing. I wanted first of all to show that this way of reasoning about catastrophe had a history, in which the eighteenth century holds a leading place. Second, and above all, I wished to examine the link between catastrophe and evil by bringing to bear an argument developed by Susan Neiman, an authority on Kant and a disciple of Hannah Arendt, as part of a larger view of the history of Western philosophy as an extended exercise in thinking about evil.[19] Neiman analyzes the evolution of our notions of natural evil and moral evil, and the complex relations between them, with great subtlety. Lisbon, Auschwitz, and 11 September figure prominently among the catastrophes she considers. Her crucial insight, borrowed from Arendt, is that when moral evil attains its height, as at Auschwitz, the categories that we habitually rely on to make moral judgments in ordinary life are shattered. In that case evil can be accounted for only in terms of an attack on the *natural* order of the world, with the result that the foundations of enlightened doomsaying are strengthened and reinforced. For this kind of explanation is a piece of metaphysical cunning that makes it possible to do away with some part of the responsibility we would otherwise bear, by converting evil into fate, into a secular form of transcendence, as it were. This overarching and supernatural phenomenon is utterly devoid of malicious intent. It is nonetheless extremely dangerous—and yet there is a chance it may leave us alone so long as we do not openly defy it. The evil represented by the Kyoto of my title—the flood to come—is all the more readily imagined in these terms as Auschwitz has already been conceived in this way, and since the minimal intentionality embodied by Kyoto quite obviously bears no comparison to the deliberate slaughter carried out at Auschwitz.

I had almost finished writing my lecture when the Asian tsunami struck on 26 December 2004. I had to banish from my mind the terrible thought that each time I complete a work on the subject, a major catastrophe is magically bound to strike. Once the astonishment of another such coincidence had worn off, however, I was confronted with a rather different kind of shock. It sprang from the unexpected nature of the world's reaction to the event.

At first, despite the scale of the disaster and the vast human suffering it had caused, I found a certain innocence in it. Finally, I said to myself, a purely natural catastrophe, one that cannot possibly be suspected of concealing human turpitude and depravity. Typhoons, hurricanes, tornados, violent storms, rising seas, torrential rains, floods, avalanches, heat waves, drought, episodes of intense cold—all these things, which formerly were regarded as manifestations of the force of nature, are now liable to be ascribed to the destruction unthinkingly wrought by mankind on this same natural world. But an earthquake beneath the sea? Surely it would be the height of presumption to think that we could have anything to do with such a thing! I was quickly disillusioned. The deafening noise of journalistic opinion, the garrulous, pointless, and sometimes indecent competition to give proofs of compassionate feeling, the shameless search for partisan advantage in deciphering the meaning of the event all seemed to recall an age that one might have been forgiven for supposing was long past—the one that witnessed the Lisbon earthquake. It was altogether as if in the meantime, from Lisbon in 1755 to Sumatra in 2004, we had learned nothing about evil.

Naturally I was asked by the press to comment on the events in Asia. My first instinct was to say that I had nothing to add, because my research was concerned with catastrophes for which mankind is directly or indirectly to blame. *Natural* catastrophes, however tragic their consequences might be, do not come within the purview of the philosophical method that I call enlightened doomsaying. But it soon became clear to me that this was a poor excuse. There was no way to overlook the inconsistency between, on the one hand, my insistence on regarding future catastrophe in the manner of destiny or fate, while holding that it is something that we remain free to avoid, and, on the other hand, the troubling tendency of commentators on the upheaval of the Indian Ocean to find human intention everywhere, even in the tsunami itself. That, as we shall see, was precisely Rousseau's reaction to the Lisbon earthquake. But nothing exceeded the incomprehension displayed by a French environmental group specializing in the study of natural catastrophe that resolved in the name of enlightened doomsaying to banish the very expression "natural catastrophe" from its vocabulary (and also from its own name). It gave the following reason:

> A natural risk is characterized by the combination of *chance* (that is, the generative geological phenomenon) with *vulnerability* (the effect on the built environment). Many major earthquakes go unnoticed when they strike uninhabited regions. The characteristic feature of risk today, in terms of its impact, what makes [a natural event] a catastrophe, is the [degree of] *human exposure*. It is for this reason that one of the results of the International Decade for Natural Disaster Reduction [IDNDR], which ended in 2000, was agreement that one should no longer speak of "natural catastrophe." *While unpreventable natural hazards do exist, it is social vulnerability that transforms such phenomena into catastrophes.*[20]

Some misunderstandings are the result simply of being distracted, or of failing to pay attention; others signal the existence of deep conceptual confusions. In trying to get to the bottom of such confusions it sometimes happens that we come upon profound insights. This is what I hope may be the result of the present essay. I see more clearly today that the chief obstacle standing in the way of enlightened doomsaying, both as an attitude and as a method of reasoning, has to do with what at the outset I called the metaphysical arrogance of the modern world. Everything that is a part of the finiteness of human beings has now been reduced to the status of a problem that science and technology will, with enough ingenuity, sooner or later make go away. Not only nature, when it thwarts our ambitions, but death itself is now seen as a problem to be solved.[21] Yet mankind, reduced to mere problem-solving, cannot know what destiny is; as *Homo faber*, it must be ignorant of contingency. Our dreams of achieving mastery and control over life bid fair to breed monsters that will devour us all in the end.

CHAPTER 2

From Lisbon to Sumatra

Jesus answered . . . "Or those eighteen on whom the tower in Siloam fell and killed them, do you think that they were worse sinners than all other men who dwelt in Jerusalem?"

—Luke 13:4

Like the furiously darting tongue of a frog seizing an insect with lightning speed, the ocean's tidal wave rushed over the shore and snatched its prey in an instant. The thing happened so quickly, psychologists tell us, that survivors scarcely knew what hit them. "The shock caused by a tsunami is of a quite specific kind," one of them explained. "Unlike a storm or a typhoon, there is no warning: it's a beautiful day, a wave comes, and after that there's nothing left."[1]

Once again, one was reduced to quantitative comparisons in trying to make sense of calamitous misfortune. In the eighteenth century, war was the preeminent symbol and measure of massive destruction. One writer sought to console the victims of the Lisbon earthquake by comparing it to a conquering army that leaves behind only ruin and desolation. Two and a half centuries later, human powers of annihilation having in the meantime become infinitely greater than what they were then, the Sumatra earthquake of December 2004 was still being likened to an act of intentional destruction, not only in order to give some idea of the monstrous scale of the cataclysm, but also to emphasize the powerlessness of human beings against it. According to one scientist, the devastation was the equivalent of exploding thirty thousand atomic bombs;[2] according to a former French president, of exploding a hundred nuclear devices.[3] Presumably the one was talking of fission weapons, the other of thermonuclear bombs. Whereas the bombs used against Hiroshima and Nagasaki killed or horribly mutilated more than two hundred thousand people in the blink of an eye, the victims of a thermonuclear war today would number in the tens or hundreds of millions. Nature has been left far behind! When one hears someone (in the event, a geophysicist) say that the Asian tsunami was "inhuman" in its scope and effects, there are good grounds for believing that he does not know what he is talking about.[4] For when it comes to sheer destructive force, human beings have become much stronger than nature. All those who seek to impress upon us the precariousness of mankind's place in the world overlook the fact that the human race has no need of tsunamis to destroy itself; it blithely applies itself to this task using its own more effective methods. One thinks, too, of another French geophysicist (a former socialist minister for education and an outspoken climate-change denier) who hastened to take advantage of the occasion to score political points against environmentalists. The Indian Ocean earthquake, he claimed, refutes the idea that nature is good.[5] But his fellow scientists tell us that an earthquake of magnitude 9 on the Richter scale in this part of the world occurs on average once every 250 years. However devastating such a natural hazard may be in its local or even regional effects, it pales in comparison with the cataclysm that we are preparing for ourselves by poisoning the atmosphere of our planet—an event not only of far graver consequence, but also one of certain, rather than more or less remote, probability. And yet few people seem to be bothered by it!

One might with rather greater justice have compared the 11 September 2001 attacks to the Lisbon earthquake, as quite a few commentators did. A calm morning, a cloudless sky, and then, out of the blue, without a hint of warning, without any public declaration of vengeance, the mortal blow. And yet, in spontaneously calling the site of the disaster "Ground Zero," Americans made it plain that it was the memory of Hiroshima that leaped to mind.

In a world filled with meaning, the one that interests me here—not the world of causes and effects studied by science—all such quantitative comparisons are sadly beside the point. The tsunami that struck in the twenty-first century revived arguments that had preoccupied philosophers during the eighteenth century, both before and after Lisbon, in connection with the nature of evil. We no longer speak of physical evil and of moral evil, as they did then. That the same word should be applied to both a tidal wave and to a war no longer makes sense to us; indeed it is just this that makes us moderns. We have learned to make a fundamental distinction between the natural world and the world of human freedom and reason: the latter is filled with intentions, whereas there are none in the former. Above all, we do not believe that what we no longer call physical evil has any link whatever with moral evil, and still less that the first type of evil should be considered just punishment for the second, in the best of all possible worlds.

Leibniz

And yet it was not so very long ago that human beings still talked and reasoned in this way, that death, sickness, and accidental injury were held to be rightfully inflicted by God on all who sin against Him—this in accordance with the principle of the summum bonum, or highest good, which God's perfection obliges him to bring about. On that view, God is the cause of physical evil. The question arose, then, whether He is also the cause of sin and of moral evil; and, if so, how He could have invented the very thing that corrupts His creation. The attempt to vindicate God's will was called theodicy in Greek, and it is this term that is traditionally used to refer to all human attempts to justify the existence of evil in a world that has been perfectly made. Saint Augustine's response is well known: God did not wish for moral evil to be; but He could not have done otherwise than to permit it, for, in creating man in His image, He created him free, and therefore free to choose evil.

This argument was widely attacked. The most formidable assault came from the Calvinist philosopher and theologian Pierre Bayle, author of a monumental *Historical and Critical Dictionary* (1695–1697). If I wish to utterly ruin someone, Bayle mockingly retorted, nothing is easier than to

20 Chapter Two

make him a gift (in this case, free will) with which he will ruin himself. The German philosopher and mathematician Gottfried Wilhelm Leibniz undertook to defend Augustine against Bayle in a pair of works that form the twin pillars of his metaphysics: the first, published in French in 1710, was a volume of essays on the goodness of God, the freedom of man, and the origin of evil titled *Theodicy*; the second, the *Monadology*, followed four years later. These treatises are no longer read, except by scholars, but their lasting fame, at least for educated readers, was assured by two volumes of philosophical tales subsequently written by Voltaire, one meant to illustrate Leibniz's theodicy (*Zadig*, 1747), the other to make a mockery of it (*Candide*, 1759). Between the two came the Lisbon earthquake.

Leibniz had argued that God's understanding comprehends an infinity of possible worlds. In deciding which one of these to bring into existence, He was prevented from choosing arbitrarily by the principle of sufficient reason, which requires that every effect have a cause. What is more, God could only choose the best world, again by virtue of the principle of the summum bonum, from which it follows that only that which displays the greatest possible degree of perfection can exist. Does this principle of the best, as it is also known, mean that God could not have chosen otherwise? No, for the necessity that guided his decision was only moral, and not metaphysical; in other words, there would not have been any logical contradiction in God's choosing another world than the best one. Yet in order to bring about the best of all possible worlds, God was obliged to leave some measure of evil in it; without this residuum our world would have been less perfect overall. Everyone today is familiar with the notion of a "necessary evil," that is, a deadly act that maximizes the general welfare (killing an innocent person, for example, in order to minimize the total number of innocents killed). An act of this sort is evil only from the finite point of view of the individual; from the point of view of the totality, it is a sacrifice for the greatest good of the community as a whole. Evil is therefore an illusion, a mere perspectival effect.

The doctrine of metaphysical optimism, as this version of theodicy is also known (where "optimism" has its classical sense, referring to the best possible state of affairs rather than a hopeful attitude toward the future),[6] was shattered on 1 November 1755 by an earthquake of scarcely lesser magnitude than that of the Sumatra earthquake of 26 December 2004. Raging fires came afterward, in Lisbon and elsewhere, extinguished finally by a gigantic

tsunami that unleashed waves fifteen meters high as far away as the shores
of Morocco and annihilated the Portuguese capital. From this catastrophe
there issued two views of evil, which posterity has associated with the names
of Voltaire and Rousseau. In March 1756, Voltaire published a philosophical
essay in verse, *Poem on the Lisbon Disaster*, to which Rousseau replied with
a *Letter to Monsieur de Voltaire*, dated 18 August of the same year. Voltaire
never responded to Rousseau directly. His answer was to be found instead
in *Candide*.

It is no part of my purpose here to give a detailed account of the dispute between Voltaire and Rousseau regarding Leibniz's theodicy. It will
be enough that we examine the reaction of our own time to the Sumatra
earthquake. In one way, of course, it was quite different from the reaction to
the Lisbon earthquake. And yet, in a deeper sense, the resemblance between
the two is astounding.

One might have expected theodicy to be absent from a world that no
longer believes itself to have been created in accordance with the principle
of the best. But the opposite was true. In Europe there was a great deal of
concern over the situation in Thailand, although the number of victims there
turned out to be considerably less than in other countries affected by the
catastrophe, no doubt because half of these victims were European tourists.
In Thailand itself the event was experienced in a very different way. Partly this
is because the country's model of economic growth, which depends to a large
degree on aggressively promoting tourism, has come under attack as a result
of the environmental threats posed by unrestrained urbanization in coastal
areas, deforestation of the interior, and all those other evils that, alas, are
now common to all other parts of the world as well. "These tidal waves were
certainly not the result of human activity," one expert allowed, "but many
people in Asia [nevertheless] interpret them *as an act of revenge by nature
and as a divine warning*."[7] These people have certainly never read Leibniz.
We may therefore be sure that theodicy is a universal human response in the
face of extreme adversity.

The same thing is regularly found in the case of terrorism, whose blind
violence mimics an earthquake's indifference to fine moral distinctions.
When a recent French prime minister declared that the release of French
hostages in Lebanon was a tribute to his country's Middle East policy; when
one of his predecessors expressed outrage that the attack on a synagogue in

the Rue Copernic in Paris, in 1980, struck "innocent passersby" (code for non-Jews)—what conception of the world informed their thinking if not the best-possible-world view, which is violated when physical harm and suffering are not distributed in proportion to what is taken to be the moral unworthiness of victims? As for those French intellectuals who saw 11 September 2001 as a day when Americans merely got what they deserved, who cried—like Leibniz, in the words of Voltaire—"God is avenged, the price of their crimes is death," they have equally proven that their thinking about evil has not advanced beyond Leibniz's ideas of theodicy.

Rousseau

In France, at least with regard to the Asian tsunami of 2004, it is the spirit of Rousseau that has by and large prevailed. What most newspaper columnists and radio and television commentators had to say about this catastrophe was already contained for the most part in this celebrated passage of the *Letter to Monsieur de Voltaire*:

> The just defense of myself obliges me only to have you observe, that in depicting human miseries, my purpose was excusable, and even praiseworthy, as I believe, *for I showed men how they caused their misfortunes themselves, and consequently how they might avoid them.*
>
> I do not see that one can seek the source of moral evil other than in man, free, perfected, thereby corrupted; and as for physical ills, . . . they are inevitable in any system of which man is a part; and then the question is not at all why is man not perfectly happy, but why does he exist? Moreover I believe I have shown that with the exception of death, which is an evil almost solely because of the preparations which one makes preceding it, *most of our physical ills are still our own work.* Without departing from your subject of Lisbon, admit, for example, that nature did not construct twenty thousand homes of six to seven stories there, and that if the inhabitants of this great city had been more equally spread out and more lightly lodged, the damage would have been much less, and perhaps of no account. All of them would have fled at the first disturbance, and the next day they would have been seen twenty leagues from there, as gay as if nothing had

happened; but it is necessary to remain, to be obstinate about some hovels, to expose oneself to new quakes, because what is left behind is worth more than what can be brought along. How many unfortunate people have perished in this disaster because of one wanting to take his clothes, another his papers, another his money? Is it not known that the person of each man has become the least part of himself, and that it is almost not worth the trouble of saving it when one has lost all the rest?

You would have wished (and who would not have wished the same) that the quake had occurred in the middle of a wilderness rather than in Lisbon. Can one doubt that such also do take place in the wildernesses? But we do not speak of them, because they do not cause any harm to the Gentlemen of the Cities, the only men of whom we take account. . . . But what does such a privilege signify? Should it be said then that the order of the world ought to change according to our whims, that nature ought to be subjugated to our laws, and that in order to interdict an earthquake in some place, we have only to build a City there?[8]

Rousseau seems not to have grasped the implication of his own argument. As against Voltaire, he intends to defend Leibnizian optimism and the goodness of Providence, but in truth he denies Providence the main part of its field of application. Moral evil, he holds, is the responsibility of human beings, and theirs alone; as for physical evil, the suffering it inflicts would be greatly lessened if society were organized differently than it is. For the path cleared by Rousseau to lead on into modernity, one last obstacle needed to be removed, by dispensing with the hypothesis of Providence, or God, and substituting in its place mankind. Of evil there would then remain only moral evil, for which only human beings could be held accountable.

The innocence that first attended the earthquake off the coast of Sumatra lasted only a few days. Again and again, of course, it was granted that no catastrophe could have been more natural; but even this certainty soon began to erode and then, finally, fell apart. For if the coral reefs and the coastal mangroves had not been ruthlessly destroyed by urbanization, aquaculture, and climate change, we were assured, they would have slowed the advance of the deadly tidal wave and significantly reduced the scope of the disaster.

Next came a moment of surpassing irony in the global media coverage of the event, when the awkward question arose why anyone should have taken such an interest in it to begin with. It did not take long for a satisfactory answer to be found: the earthquake did not occur in a desert, which is to say in an obscure corner of the Third World, like the one that had struck the Iranian city of Bam the year before, but in places that were frequented by Rousseau's "Gentlemen of the Cities," who today are called tourists. Very quickly the tsunami came to be seen as a sort of stooge, or underling, a mere accomplice of processes that are wholly social in character—processes that, in combination, cause injustice inexorably to increase in the world. Once again, the wretched of the earth were bound to be the victims. It will, of course, be difficult to use the same argument when the "Big One" destroys the San Francisco Bay Area, home to some of the wealthiest people on the planet. In the case of the Asian catastrophe, critics on the left delighted in pointing out that the Thai authorities had almost immediately been informed of the occurrence of the earthquake and of the probability of a tsunami, and that they had nevertheless decided not to announce a state of emergency for fear of harming the country's reputation as a premier tourist destination. Technical experts followed close on their heels. It did not take long for them to identify the source of the evil—ignorance, which is to say insufficient technical expertise—and the guilty parties—governments that had failed to devote enough resources to geoscience.[9] Moral evil had now managed once and for all to dispose of the last remnants of natural evil, more surely even than the tidal wave itself had swept away all that stood in its path.

Voltaire

I must confess that reading the American press on this subject seemed like a breath of fresh air. It was not less Voltairean in spirit than the French press was Rousseauist—an immense paradox, at least if one believes that Voltaire destroyed optimism. For what people on earth is more optimistic than the Americans?

Voltaire's reply to Rousseau concluded with these famous words:

And Pangloss sometimes said to Candide, "All events are linked in the best of all possible worlds. After all, had you not been chased from a fine castle

with hard kicks to your backside for love of Mademoiselle Cunégonde, had
you not been brought before the Inquisition, had not walked the length
and breadth of the Americas on foot, not run your sword through the
baron, not lost all your sheep of the fine land of El Dorado you would not
be [sitting here now] eating candied citrons and pistachios." "That is well
said," Candide replied, "but we must cultivate our garden."[10]

The influential opinion of the literary critic and historian Gustave Lanson,
that Voltaire thus fatally undermined Leibniz's doctrine, has long been
uncritically accepted—though in *Candide* he asserts no counterclaim in
this regard. One must look instead to Voltaire's reflections on the Lisbon
disaster, which bear the subtitle "Examen de cet axiome, *Tout est bien*."[11] The
reference here is to another poem, Alexander Pope's *An Essay on Man*, published in London in 1734, which Voltaire had earlier imitated in his *Discourse
on Man* (1738). His *Poem on the Lisbon Disaster* is therefore presented as a
commentary on optimism in the form given it by Pope. Now, the first of the
four epistles that comprise the *Essay on Man* concludes with these words:
"whatever is, is right," which Voltaire mistranslates by the phrase "tout est
bien."[12] Although Pope was commonly regarded as a foremost representa-
tive of optimism, Voltaire nonetheless correctly perceived that the English
poet was much closer to Pierre Bayle, whom he himself admired, than to
Leibniz, whose metaphysical dogmatism he found irritating. In his *Dictionary*, Bayle had shown that one cannot without contradiction simultaneously
affirm the following three propositions: (1) Evil exists in the world; (2) God
is benevolent; (3) God is almighty. The first proposition is undeniably a fact;
but giving up either the second or the third leads to intolerable antinomies.
If benevolence is assumed, it follows that God is not almighty and that He
must struggle against a contrary principle, Evil or Satan, without ever being
certain of victory. This is what Rousseau calls the "vile" doctrine of the Man-
ichaeans. The alternative, that God is almighty but not benevolent, is the one
he was later to ascribe to Voltaire:

What does your poem now tell me? "Suffer forever, wretches. If there is
a God who has created you, no doubt he is omnipotent; he could have
prevented all your ills: do not hope then that they will ever end; for one

would not know how to see why you exist, if it is not to suffer and die." I do not know what such a doctrine could possess that is more consoling than optimism and even fatalism. As for me, I acknowledge it appears to me even crueler than Manichaeism. If perplexity concerning the origin of evil forces you to alter one of the perfections of God, why do you wish to justify his power at the expense of his goodness? If it is necessary to choose between two errors, I like the first one even better.[13]

But Voltaire does not choose, any more than Bayle did—and this is what Rousseau fails to see. Determined not to sacrifice any of the constituent propositions of his trilemma, Bayle decided instead to sacrifice reason to faith. Pope followed Bayle in condemning the arrogance of all those who claim to be able to decipher the order of the cosmos. This is what Voltaire liked in Pope. In the preface to his poem on the Lisbon disaster, Voltaire makes it abundantly clear that he "does not take issue with the illustrious Pope, whom he has always loved and admired: he agrees with him in almost every particular." At the end of this same preface, he says this of Bayle, once again leaving no room for doubt as to his meaning: "[The author of this poem] acknowledges, with all mankind, that there is evil as well as good to be found on this earth; he admits that no philosopher has ever explained the nature of moral and physical evil; he admits that Bayle, the greatest dialectician who has ever written, has taught us only how to doubt, and that he contradicts himself; and he owns that man's understanding is as weak as his existence is miserable."[14] And in the poem itself one finds these lines:

> Leibniz does not tell me by what invisible bonds,
> In the best ordered of all possible worlds,
> An eternal disorder, a chaos of misfortunes,
> Entwines our vain pleasures with real sufferings,
> Nor why the innocent and the guilty both
> Should submit equally to this inevitable evil.
> I cannot conceive how it could be that all is good:
> I am like a doctor of philosophy; alas! I know
>   nothing.[15]

And further on:

What then can even the most immense mind know?
Nothing: the book of fate is closed to our sight.

These last lines, in which Voltaire frankly recognizes human finitude, admitting the ignorance of mankind and accepting the cruel contingencies of fate, owe little to metaphysical belief. They spring from Voltaire's most deeply held personal conviction, that every other option can have the effect only of stifling compassion:

Tranquil spectators, intrepid spirits,
Contemplating the shipwrecks of your dying brethren,
Peaceably you seek the causes of the storm:
But when you feel fate's malevolent blows,
You become more human, like us you weep.

One is put in mind of the famous *baccalauréat* examination question inviting candidates to comment on Goethe's aphorism: "With Voltaire, the old world comes to an end, and with Rousseau a new world begins." It is undeniable that Rousseau opened the way to modernity by unburdening God of responsibility for evil, and, in placing this onus on the shoulders of human beings, deprived the notion of physical evil of all meaning. But this does not justify us in relegating Voltaire among the ancients; on the contrary, he must be put in the company of the postmoderns, who insist on our duty to face up to the brutal reality of chance and contingency, rather than take refuge in the false consolation of rationalistic explanations. This is perhaps why the reaction to the Asian tsunami in America, unlike France, assumed a Voltairean cast.

One example must stand for many, a very fine and unsettling piece published by David Brooks in the *New York Times*, which captures the general tone of what was being written and said in the United States about the earthquake of December 2004.[16] Like Voltaire, Brooks begins by recalling that there was a time when earthquakes were explained by appeal to the justice of a God who punishes sinners with pain and misery. And like Voltaire, he finds this type of account repugnant. In the words of the philosopher:

At the half-formed cries of their dying voices,
At the terrifying sight of their smoking ashes,

Will you say: "It is the effect of eternal laws
That give a free and good God no other choice"?
Will you say, on seeing this heap of victims,
"God is avenged, the price of their crimes is death"?
What crime, what sin have these children committed,
Crushed and bleeding over their mothers' breasts?

Nevertheless, Brooks adds, at least the old explanation placed mankind at the center of history, as the object of divine will and purpose. Today, he observes, to judge from what is said about it, one has the impression that "the meaning of this event is that there is no meaning," at least no meaning that we are able to comprehend.

Some survived the cataclysm in improbable ways, bordering occasionally on the burlesque, whereas their next-door neighbors were carried away, never to be seen again. Some babies were found sitting on mattresses, unharmed, while others were snatched from the arms of their mothers. "There is no human agency in these stories," Brooks remarks, "just nature's awful lottery." Nature is inseparable from chaos, irremediably opaque to human understanding. Whatever it does, it does without reason. For a people taught by Thoreau and John Muir to romanticize nature, the tsunami was a sudden and rude awakening.

Voltaire, who was not a metaphysician, understood just this, exactly the thing that had escaped Leibniz. Imagine a tale of human adventure that obeys the principle of sufficient reason at every step along the way. It does not follow from this that the sequence of events itself, the summation of all its various moments, forms a rational and meaningful account. The episodes that make up *Candide* are masterpieces of absurdity, in which the action unfolds with no greater reason than does a tidal wave lashing out at the shore, and yet each one of the stages in the young man's travels, as enumerated by Pangloss, is causally linked to the next. In driving a wedge between reasons and causes, between causes and reasons, Voltaire anticipated the importance of the role that the concept of process was to play in twentieth-century philosophies of the physical universe.[17]

American commentary on the disaster touched on the essential aspect of Voltaire's attitude when it turned to the matter of compassion. There had been much self-congratulation in Europe, and particularly in France, with regard to the generosity shown in helping the victims of the tsunami; indeed, it was so extravagant that one humanitarian organization had to plead for a moratorium on further contributions, leading some to prophesy the advent of a worldwide spirit of solidarity. Though the limits of indecency were overstepped several times, the height of obscenity was not reached until one of the two French geophysicists I mentioned earlier took advantage of the catastrophe to call for greater investment in his branch of science, which he claimed to be uniquely qualified to protect the poorest nations against the worst effects of natural disaster: "The task before us is immense, but researchers are eager to get to work, brimming with enthusiasm and new ideas. All they lack is funding. . . . We cannot afford to be stingy. Millions of lives are at stake. Are democratic societies today . . . capable of rising to this challenge and coming to the aid of the most disadvantaged, who often pay the heaviest price?"[18] American experts had answered him in advance. "The really big money can be better and more usefully absorbed by developing good health and education programs in the poorest countries," pointed out Nancy Birdsall, president of the Center for Global Development; and as the economist Jeffrey Sachs observed, if we really want to save millions of lives per year in the developing world, the top priority should be eradicating malaria.[19] If, as seems probable, governmental assistance to the victims of the Asian tsunami will be deducted from the monies earmarked by wealthy countries for development aid, the eight million people around the world who die every year of diseases that can be prevented by simple and relatively inexpensive measures will once again have been left to their unhappy fate.[20] Generosity, after all, is not to be reckoned in terms of what is done when everyone's attention is focused on a tragedy, but when it is focused on something else, diverted by the sensation of more recent events. I read French newspapers carefully, listened to the radio and watched television, hoping to come across some hint of Voltairean irony. But I found nothing of the sort.

The lesson drawn by Voltaire in his poem on the Lisbon earthquake is unforgiving: only those who dare to look into the abyss of meaninglessness are capable of true compassion. Few people, and certainly no one in France, appreciated this more clearly than David Brooks, who concluded his column on the Sumatra earthquake with these words:

The world's generosity has indeed been amazing, but sometimes we use our compassion as a self-enveloping fog to obscure our view of the abyss. Somehow it's wrong to turn this event into a good-news story so we can all feel warm this holiday season. It's wrong to turn it into a story about us, who gave, rather than about them, whose lives were ruined. It's certainly wrong to turn this into yet another petty political spat, as many tried, disgustingly, to do.

This is a moment to feel deeply bad, for the dead and for those of us who have no explanation.[21]

It is in this attitude that true dignity and generosity of spirit are to be found. Certainly there is no optimism in it, but neither is there any pessimism. It may instead be the prolegomenon to an ethics of human finitude.

Although I found in the commentary on the Asian tsunami that appeared in France no allusion to the dispute between Voltaire and Rousseau, I did happen to come across a quotation in an article by another American journalist that perfectly conveys the gist of their quarrel—Gloucester's famous lament in the first scene of act 4 of *King Lear*: "As flies to wanton boys are we to the gods. They kill us for their sport."[22]

And people still dare to say that Americans are uncultured!

CHAPTER 3

The Naturalization of Evil

[The survivors of Hiroshima] constantly speak of the catastrophe as if it were an earthquake or a tidal wave. They use the Japanese word, *tsunami*.
—Günther Anders

Susan Neiman, whose fine book on evil in modern thought I mentioned earlier, has shown that the style of thought initiated by Rousseau was bound finally to collapse under the weight of the excessive responsibility it ascribes to human beings. If moral evil is everywhere, and if human beings must always be held accountable for it, then man has taken the place of Leibniz's God. Theodicy, in Vladimir Jankélévitch's phrase, turns into anthropodicy.[1] But obviously we do not have at our disposal the means that would allow us to make good on our claim to be God. Not only does the physical world continue to resist our attempts at mastery, notwithstanding the extraordinary effectiveness of our technologies; the moral world remains hopelessly opaque to us as well. For while it is true that we make our own history, we do not know which history we are making. In the modern history of Western philosophy, which Neiman sees as an extended exercise in thinking about evil, there is a moment of hesitation, and then a sort of turning back, with the result that responsibility for a part of what happens to us, and in particular for the crushing misfortunes to which we are liable, comes once again to be imputed to nature—not physical nature, but moral nature, as it were, which is to say a conception of the moral world modeled on nature.

Neiman detects the first stirrings of this impulse in Kant. There is a great paradox in this, for if ever there was a thinker who insisted on separating the world of nature from the world of freedom and reason, it was Kant. It is all the more remarkable, then, that in laying down the universalizing principle that is at the heart of the idea of a categorical imperative, as the law of the moral world, he should have opened the way for the natural world to make a triumphant return in commanding that each person "act only according to that maxim whereby you can, at the same time, will that it should become a universal law *of nature*." The reference to nature here, just when it was least expected, betrays an extraordinary tension. On the one hand, Neiman observes, moral law enjoins us, when we act of our own free will, to set ourselves up as legislators—not only for ourselves as individuals, but for humanity as a whole. In that case our responsibility is total. With the inclusion of nature it is magnified still further, so that now we are God's equal. But by the same token it is the world of freedom that, in a sense, gives way to the world of nature and its laws. We are relieved of our infinite responsibility at the very moment when we assume it totally.[2]

Neiman notices an analogous process of transubstantiation at work in Marx's doctrine of historical materialism. The moral indignation from which it arises leads on to a kind of transcendence that is anything but moral, since, if capitalism is doomed to dig its own grave, this will be the result of pure obedience to a natural law.[3] As Hans Jonas put it: "For political action thus determined, which makes happen what must happen, this closed circuit creates a most peculiar mixture of colossal responsibility for the future with deterministic release from responsibility."[4] There is no Marxist ethics, only a Marxist economics.

I will say nothing more of Neiman's history of the philosophy of evil, for I am interested chiefly in the role played in completing and enlarging the tendency that first came into existence with Kant by the twin moral catastrophes of the twentieth century, the destruction of European Jewry and the nuclear age inaugurated by the bombing of Hiroshima, and later, not quite a year into the present century, the terrorist attacks of 11 September 2001.

New York

On 11 September 2011, an apocalyptic event took place on American soil. I use the word "apocalypse" in its true sense, not with reference to a catastrophe that will put an end to the world, but instead to something that is a bearer of revelation. On 11 September, an aspect of evil was spectacularly revealed, if not actually created, before the eyes of the whole world, which stood and stared in disbelief, dumbfounded by what had happened. In saying this I am aware that my opinion is not universally shared.[5] I will not discuss other interpretations here, except to repeat that the number of victims is evidently not a pertinent criterion.

I gave the title "Rousseau in Manhattan" to an essay I wrote about 11 September immediately afterward,[6] for the key to understanding the moral catastrophe this event represents is to be found, I believe, in the conception of social—and therefore moral—evil bequeathed to us by the author of the *Confessions*. Up to this point I may have given the impression that I take the side of Voltaire against Rousseau. Nothing could be farther from the truth. Rousseau was a philosopher of immense importance, in my view; Voltaire, despite his unarguable brilliance, was not. Just the same, when one has been confined too long among the torments of Rousseau's wonderfully complicated mind, it is a most welcome thing, as I say, to go out for a breath of fresh air in the company of Voltaire.

There are two places where Rousseau associates catastrophe with evil. The first is a cosmic catastrophe; the second, a moral catastrophe. But it is a simple matter to show that they are identical. In the *Essay on the Origin of Languages*,[7] Rousseau presents a founding myth of society that coincides with the origin of evil:

> Mild climates, lush and fertile lands have been the first to be populated and the last where nations have been formed, because men could more easily do without one another there, and because the needs that cause society to arise made themselves felt later there.
>
> Assume a perpetual spring on earth; assume water, livestock, pasturage everywhere; assume men leaving the hands of nature, once dispersed throughout all this: I cannot imagine how they would ever have renounced their primitive freedom and forsaken the isolated and pastoral life so suited

to their natural indolence, in order needlessly to impose on themselves the slavery, the labors, the miseries and poverty inseparable from the social state.

He who willed that man be sociable touched his finger to the axis of the globe and inclined it at an angle to the axis of the universe. With this slight movement I see the face of the earth change and the vocation of mankind decided: I hear from afar the joyous cries of a senseless multitude; I see Palaces and Towns raised; I see the arts, laws, commerce born; I see peoples forming, extending, dissolving, succeeding one another like the waves of the sea: I see men gathered together at a few dwelling places in order to devour each other there, to make a frightful desert of the rest of the world; a worthy monument to social union and the usefulness of the arts.[8]

Note well this line: "He who willed that man be sociable touched his finger to the axis of the globe and inclined it at an angle to the axis of the universe." Society first appeared, then, as a consequence of an event in the physical world—even if, as one might suspect, the owner of the cosmic finger was none other than God himself. Note, too, this remarkable irony in our own time: the Sumatra earthquake was later discovered to have unleashed such force that it actually tilted the earth's axis of rotation with respect to the ecliptic plane—only to an infinitesimal extent, to be sure, something like one ten-millionth of a degree; but tilted it nonetheless. Let us not mistake Rousseau's real motive in telling us this tale, however. What he wants us to understand is that the transition from *amour de soi* to *amour-propre* was a necessary condition of human society and that it could not *not* have occurred. Rousseau does not use the word "catastrophe" in this connection, but I am more than happy to do so—without fear of anachronism, for I use it in the sense it acquired in the mathematical and physical sciences during the second half of the twentieth century. A catastrophe is the occurrence of an abrupt discontinuity in a system characterized by continuous dynamics. Consider a highway that is approaching a point of saturation, in the sense that it is carrying nearly the maximum load for which it was designed. A single, apparently insignificant event—one car bumping into another, say—is enough to suddenly immobilize the flow of traffic, as though it were trapped in a sort of gel. The immediate cause is, strictly speaking, of no importance: any other such event—an accident on one side of the road that distracts the attention of drivers headed in the opposite direction, for example—would have produced the same effect. In Rousseau, *amour de soi*, which closes each individual in upon himself, each one "regarding himself as the sole Spectator to observe him, as the sole being in the universe to take an interest in him, and as the sole judge of his own merit," and "seeing his fellows hardly otherwise than he would see Animals of another species"[9]—this feeling, synonymous in Rousseau's account with goodness and benevolence, is structurally unstable in the same manner. The least flick of a finger, no matter that it may be a cosmic finger, is enough to cause a person to bring forth what he carries inside him—while at the same time containing it in another sense, of holding it in check. This is *amour-propre*, through which evil befalls humanity. It comes into existence when another person comes near enough that our gaze crosses with his and we begin to compare ourselves to each other; for when "men begin to cast their eyes upon their fellows . . . , their interests cross each other . . . [and] *amour de soi*, put into fermentation, changes into *amour-propre*."[10] *Amour-propre* gives rise to the sidelong glance—etymologically, envy, the invidious look (Latin *invidia*, from the verbal form meaning "to cast an evil eye upon")—that "comes from the desire always to be transported out of ourselves."[11] Rousseau—the philosopher who exclaimed, "Man, seek the author of evil no longer. It is yourself. No evil exists other than that which you do or suffer, and both come to you from yourself"[12]—is the last one to be fooled by his own myth of cosmic or divine origin. The hesitation and ambivalence found in the *Letter to Voltaire* of 1756 are now gone: evil has become purely and simply moral.

Rousseau had personal, and very painful, experience of evil. Later he did in fact use the word "catastrophe" (more precisely, "my catastrophe"—the stoning of his house at Môtiers), in book 12 of the *Confessions*, where he described the "heartache" that he felt at the "spectacle of the people's hatred" in great detail.[13] To Michel Serres we owe a splendid commentary on this passage:

When he was writing of the social pact, no contradiction bothered him; everything seemed crystal clear to him. It seemed transparent to go back to a first convention; it seemed evident to him that an act of association would produce a group ego or a public persona. Today, those plotting against me, those in league together, form, he says, an indissoluble body whose members can no longer be separated [from one another]. In the political sense, they form a republic. Rousseau sees that what he had foreseen is now constituted, but he is [looking from] outside; he sees a dispersed set form a unit, a unanimous gathering of forces—and it all seems obscure to him.

The truth is that he is right; the truth is that he made decisive progress in politics. . . . General will is rare and perhaps only theoretical. General hatred is frequent and is part of the practical world. . . . Not only does he see the formation of a social pact from the outside, not only does he notice the formation of a general will, but he also observes, through the darkness, that it is formed only through animosity, that it is formed only because he is its victim. . . . Union is produced through expulsion. And he is the one who is expelled.[14]

Rousseau demystified the evil that exists in the best of all possible worlds—metaphysical evil—by revealing its anthropological foundation: order is built up on the backs of scapegoats. In the collective process of victimization, each person finds in the hateful regard that others cast upon the scapegoat a sufficient reason to hate the scapegoat himself.

Have I lost the thread of my argument here? Not at all! But before coming back to 11 September, I must prolong the detour just a bit further. Let us consider a variant of the famous master-slave dialectic—the argument that Hegel contrived to persuade himself that there is reason in history, albeit reason of a cunning sort[15]—in which *amour-propre* is substituted for the desire for recognition. Such desire is only a particular case of *amour-propre*, neither its ultimate source nor even its most significant manifestation. The details of my story are irrelevant. It might take place in a school yard or on the world stage: whether it is a quarrel over who has the smartest smartphone or a race to acquire the latest nuclear weapons, one person is competing with another to be the first to get hold of a certain object. As the struggle intensifies, the object of their dispute loses its importance—to the point, finally, that it no longer matters at all.[16] The adversaries are still fighting over something, or so they imagine anyway; in fact they are fighting over what they call "face," or "prestige"—which is to say (as the etymology of the latter term reminds us) over nothing, and for no reason. They are in the grips of a very powerful illusion. Their mutual animosity continues to grow, the hatred of the one being ratcheted up to new heights by the hatred of the other, with the result that they soon become inseparable.[17] No object any longer stands between them, nothing that might keep them from destroying each other and the world around them. It would be altogether misleading to speak of nihilism in this case, however.[18] For then one remains the captive of a conception of human behavior that explains action in terms of reasons, in terms of desires and beliefs. On this view, the nihilist must still desire something, namely, nothingness. Once again it is Rousseau who has shown us why a more penetrating analysis is needed. On the nature of hatred, I know of nothing truer, nothing more profound or more disturbing, than this passage in the *Dialogues* (also known as *Rousseau, Judge of Jean-Jacques*—a sequel to the *Confessions*, as it were):

> The primitive passions, which all tend directly toward our happiness, focus us only on objects that relate to it, and having only *amour de soi* as a principle, are all loving and gentle in their essence. But when, being *deflected from their object by obstacles, they focus on removing the obstacle rather than on reaching the object*, then their nature changes and they become irascible and hateful. And that is how *amour de soi*, which is a good and absolute feeling, becomes *amour-propre*, which is to say a relative feeling by which one makes comparisons; the latter feeling demands preferences, and its enjoyment is purely negative, as it no longer seeks satisfaction in our own benefit but solely in the harm of another.[19]

Much attention has been given, and still continues to be given today, to the objectives that were pursued by the authors of the attacks of 11 September and to the strategy they followed. Commentators have looked to the beliefs of the terrorists themselves for the source of the mental strength that enabled them to undertake such monstrous acts; extenuating circumstances have sometimes been invoked, on the ground that these men had the courage to sacrifice their lives for the sake of a conviction. In all of this it has not been understood that the Twin Towers in Manhattan were not the highjackers' objective, but the irresistibly fascinating obstacle that attracted them like moths to a flame.

What has not been grasped, in other words, is the true nature of hatred. We make it seem more humane than it actually is, more amenable to reason, by believing that it had an object in this case and that the authors of the crime had reasons. The causes of their acts have been mistaken for reasons, once more in disregard of Voltaire's teaching. The causes of 11 September are many, and they can be endlessly debated. Our usual ways of speaking encourage us to convert a cause, in the sense of an efficient cause, into a "cause," in the moral sense of the term. But this is because our language itself has not properly appreciated how extreme evil really is.

◆   ◆   ◆

Rousseau's influence in the history of modern thought can scarcely be overestimated. It is owing to him that we have come to believe that evil is completely and entirely the responsibility of human beings; that there is no natural or physical evil. It is this conviction that forms the basis for the separation we go on adamantly trying to enforce between the world of nature, having neither intentions nor reasons, uniquely populated by causes, and the world of freedom, where reasons for acting come under the jurisdiction of moral law. But it is the same Rousseau who has made us understand that extreme evil shatters the bulwarks we have built to protect ourselves against the collapse of the moral world and its descent into the realm of natural processes and physical mechanisms.

I am aware, of course, that everything I have just rehearsed at such length is contained in a single biblical phrase, found in the Psalms (69:4) as well as the Gospels (John 15:25): "They hated me for no reason."[20]

Auschwitz

The two greatest monstrosities bequeathed to us by the twentieth century, the Shoah and the nuclear threat, have this in common, that they hurled moral evil headlong into the world of nature. Before Lisbon even earthquakes were a species of moral evil, since they punished an ethical transgression. Now, in the age heralded by Auschwitz and Hiroshima, the deliberate murder of tens of millions of innocent people has come to be seen as a fact of nature. But how could it have been otherwise? Nothing in what we call morality or ethics is capable of bearing the enormity of the evil that darkened the century we have just left behind. Satan himself would not be sufficient unto this new day—that poor devil who, in the figure of Goethe's Mephistopheles, ever means evil but always does good.[21]

The book that Hannah Arendt wrote about Adolf Eichmann's trial in Jerusalem provoked unprecedented outrage and controversy. The unintended hurt it caused, even to her friends, is well worth pondering.[22] In the epilogue Arendt said this:

> Foremost among the larger issues at stake in the Eichmann trial was the assumption current in all modern legal systems that intent to do wrong is necessary for the commission of a crime. On nothing, perhaps, has civilized jurisprudence prided itself more than on this taking into account of the subjective factor. Where this intent is absent, where, for whatever reasons, even reasons of moral insanity, the ability to distinguish between right and wrong is impaired, we feel no crime has been committed. We refuse, and consider as barbaric, the propositions "that a great crime offends nature, so that the very earth cries out for vengeance; that evil violates a natural harmony which only retribution can restore; that a wronged collectivity owes a duty to the moral order to punish the criminal" (Yosal Rogat). And yet I think it is undeniable that it was precisely on the ground of these long-forgotten propositions that Eichmann was brought to justice to begin with, and that they were, in fact, the supreme justification for the death penalty.[23]

The zealous high commissioner of the Final Solution described in *Eichmann in Jerusalem* is anything but a bloodthirsty monster. Eichmann did not wish to do evil. He simply did not realize what he was doing. His ambitions were modest—to be looked upon favorably by his superiors, to do his job well. For want of a moral conscience (*Gewissen*), he was conscientious (*gewissenhaft*). And yet he was by no means an ordinary person. A few singular traits set him apart from the common run of mortals, and predisposed him to become one of the greatest criminals of all time: a total lack of imagination; an incapacity to put himself in the place of others, to see the world through their eyes; and what Arendt calls "thoughtlessness"—the fact that, as it might well be said, he could not see further than the end of his own nose.

What so many found shocking was the idea that extreme ordinariness could have coincided with so vast an evil. Arendt was accused by some of seeking to absolve Eichmann of the full weight of his crime. This complaint failed to take notice of an essential detail that Arendt had introduced in the 1965 postscript to her work, in an unsuccessful attempt to clear up all misunderstanding: "That such remoteness from reality and such thoughtlessness can wreak more havoc than all the evil instincts taken together which, perhaps, are inherent in man—that was, in fact, the lesson one could learn in Jerusalem. *But it was a lesson, neither an explanation of the phenomenon nor a theory about it.*"[24]

A lesson, and not an explanation. The distinction is of the highest importance. There is no shortage of explanations, beginning with the one offered by Eichmann and his lawyers: he was only a "tiny cog" in a vast administrative machinery, a mere bureaucrat who was only following orders. Arendt concedes that a sociological theory of bureaucracy or of totalitarian regimes might disclose the causal factors that account for the behavior of a man such as Eichmann. But in a criminal trial, the accused, however dehumanizing the circumstances that may have led him to commit the crime with which he is charged, is treated as a human being, not as a cog in a machine. "If the defendant excuses himself on the ground that he acted not as a man but as a mere functionary whose functions could just as easily have been carried out by anyone else, it is as if a criminal pointed to the statistics on crime—which set forth that so-and-so many crimes per day are committed in such-and-such a place—and declared that he only did what was statistically expected, that it was mere accident he did it and not somebody else, since after all somebody had to do it."[25]

There can be no disputing that Arendt held Eichmann fully responsible for his crimes. Only the death penalty seemed to her an adequate remedy in this instance. Normally, blame is to be sought not in the causal mechanisms that produce a crime, but in the reasons the accused had for committing it; not on the side of nature, but on the side of freedom. But there are no such reasons in the case of Eichmann, for the distance that separates the freedom of the accused from the consequences of his acts is the same one that separates zero from infinity. We must therefore resign ourselves to an intolerable paradox, that our responsibility with regard to the natural order of the world is limitless. That is the meaning of the passage from Arendt's epilogue I quoted a moment ago: at this point, there is no longer any moral evil; human crimes are now cosmic in scale.

In the meantime, Arendt noted, some German churches had asked forgiveness for not having shown enough compassion, enough *mercy* for the victims of Nazi genocide. But mercy is the goodness that moves God to pardon men their sins and, by extension, the generosity that inspires us to pardon a criminal for his crime; it is the indulgence freely shown toward a vanquished adversary. Were these victims guilty of anything? By an obscene "slip of the tongue," mercy has been confused with justice.[26] For it is justice that a wounded earth demands, so that the natural order of things may be restored.

The incomprehension with which Arendt's book was met at the time, especially among Jewish intellectuals, resonates still today in the reaction of authors such as Richard Wolin:

> The most forceful *accusation* Arendt could mobilize against Eichmann and his fellow perpetrators was the charge of "thoughtlessness"—a characterization that seriously misapprehended the nature of Nazi ideology, its power as an all-encompassing worldview. In Arendt's view, the Nazis were less guilty of "crimes against humanity" than they were of "an inability to think"—a charge which, if taken at face value, risks equating their misdeeds with those of a dim-witted child.[27]

I am less interested in debating the correctness of Arendt's analysis of Nazism than in protesting the gross error of interpretation that has been committed here. When Arendt says that Eichmann suffered from shortsightedness, it is, I repeat, not a moral, much less a legal, accusation that she brings against him; she is simply describing a facet of his character, what today would be spoken of in terms of "cognitive impairment"—a minor detail, except for the enormity of the moral responsibility borne by the person who was afflicted with it in this case. What is truly difficult to comprehend, and what continues to undermine the categories we are accustomed to rely on in making sense of the world, is the idea that immense harm may be caused without the least malignity; that unimaginable guilt may go hand in hand with an utter absence of malice.

In the light of what we now know about Eichmann, Arendt does seem to have been mistaken about his motives.[28] Even so, the fantastic possibility to which she alerted us is now undeniably a part of our world. But then one runs up against another difficulty, which makes it clearer why her thesis was so abruptly dismissed: the question of the uniqueness and the incommensurability of Auschwitz. In the words of another one of her critics: "Arendt tends toward a kind of universal extremism, which derealizes historical actuality. In her mind, Auschwitz becomes possible everywhere, although it turned out to have been executed by Nazi Germany. This tendency in exposing the historical reality and the universal possibility of Auschwitz at reality's expense, is a pervading undercurrent in Hannah Arendt's argumentation. Such universalization tends to deconstruct the event—and to offend the victims."[29]

There is no question that Arendt (following Günther Anders on this point) saw the incomparable evil revealed by Auschwitz as the embodiment of a general structure ordering the dynamics of the modern world. One of the main sources of this evil is the absolute dominion technology exerts over human beings, as Arendt had seen with great acuity three years before the Eichmann trial:

> It could be that we, who are earth-bound creatures and have begun to act as though we were dwellers of the universe, will forever be unable to understand, that is, to think and speak about the things which nevertheless we are able to do. . . . If it should turn out to be true that knowledge (in the modern sense of know-how) and thought have parted company for good, then we would indeed become the helpless slaves, not so much of our machines as of our know-how, *thoughtless* creatures at the mercy of every gadget which is technically possible, no matter how murderous it is.[30]

One cannot help but be struck by the fact that Arendt uses the same word, "thoughtless," to refer both to Eichmann and to all those who exploit the power of technology.

◆　◆　◆

The director Claude Lanzmann has explained more than once his reasons for giving the name Shoah to "the thing" that forms the subject of his 1985 documentary film of the same title. The choice arose in the first instance from a refusal—a refusal to call it a "holocaust." A holocaust is a ritual sacrifice, and therefore presupposes a divinity that receives the offering constituted by the lives of the victims who have been tortured and consumed by fire. To which divinity, then, were the millions of Jewish victims sacrificed? In confusing mass murder with the expiation of sins one sacralizes barbarism, and in this way justifies it. No purer example of sacrilege can be imagined. What does the Hebrew word "*shoah*" signify? "I chose the name because I didn't understand what it meant," Lanzmann admitted in a recent interview. "It is a word that the rabbis found in the Bible after the war. *Shoah* signifies catastrophe, destruction, but *it may be a natural catastrophe as well.* The word is therefore completely inadequate, even for those who speak Hebrew. *A tsunami is a type of* shoah."[31]

Some of the catastrophe's survivors chose to obey a rule that is simple in its absoluteness: do not understand. "Bringing oneself to face horror directly," Lanzmann has written, "means having to renounce distractions and evasions, chief among these the most falsely central question—the question of why."[32]

"*Hier ist kein Warum*"—there is no why here. Thus the watchword of Auschwitz.[33] No why—only causes, as blind and as devoid of meaning as the ones that make a wave destroy a life here while sparing another there.

Hiroshima

On 6 August 1945 an atomic bomb annihilated the Japanese city of Hiroshima. Three days later, Nagasaki was destroyed. In the meantime, on 8 August, the International Military Tribunal at Nuremberg provided itself with the authority to judge three types of crime: crimes against peace, war crimes, and crimes against humanity. In the space of three days, then, the victors of the Second World War inaugurated an era in which unthinkably powerful arms of mass destruction made it inevitable that wars would now be judged criminal by the very norms that these victors were laying down at the same moment. This monstrous irony was forever to mark the thought of the most neglected German philosopher of the twentieth century, Günther Anders.

Even a panoramic survey of moral catastrophes such as this one is obliged to mention Anders, it seems to me, for he is one of the very few thinkers who have had both the courage and the lucidity to link Hiroshima with Auschwitz, without in any way depriving Auschwitz of the sad privilege it enjoys as the incarnation of bottomless moral horror. He was able to do this because he understood (as Arendt herself did, though probably somewhat later) two fundamental things: first, no matter that moral evil, beyond a certain threshold, becomes too much for human beings to bear, they nonetheless remain responsible for it; second, no ethics, no standard of rationality, no norm that human beings can establish for themselves has the least relevance in trying to make sense of such evil.

Why does it take courage and lucidity to link the two events? Because still today in the minds of many people—including, it would appear, a very large majority of Americans—Hiroshima is the classic example of a necessary evil,[34] the paradigm of anthropodicy. America, having invested itself with the power to bring into existence, if not the best of all possible worlds,[35] then at least the least bad among them, placed on one of the scales of justice the bombing of civilians and their murder in the hundreds of thousands, and on the other an invasion of the Japanese archipelago that, it was said, would have cost the lives of a half million American soldiers. Moral necessity, it was argued, required that America choose to put an end to the war as quickly as possible, even if this meant ignoring everything that until then had constituted the most elementary rules of just war. But what part did necessity play in sending millions of Jewish children from every part of Europe to be gassed?

In January 2005, with the commemoration of the sixtieth anniversary of the liberation of the Nazi extermination camps, long-forgotten emotions at once rose up again from the depths of even the most hardened hearts. Though these sentiments had never quite disappeared, the six decades since the bombing of Hiroshima had relegated them to the deepest recesses of historical memory. No more than the Saint Bartholomew's Day massacre almost four hundred years earlier, the destruction of this city was not capable of awakening in us anything more than a rather remote intellectual interest in depravities and horrors. And yet down through these decades a few vigilant keepers of the human conscience stubbornly proclaimed the inherent immorality of atomic weapons. In 1960, shortly before his death, Leo Szilard, the Hungarian-born physicist who, together with Einstein, composed the letter to President Roosevelt that was to launch the Manhattan Project, posed the following question: "Suppose [Nazi] Germany had developed two bombs before we had any bombs. And suppose Germany had dropped one bomb, say, on Rochester and the other on Buffalo, and then having run out of bombs she would have lost the war. Can anyone doubt that we would then have defined the dropping of atomic bombs on cities as a war crime, and that we would have sentenced the Germans who were guilty of this crime to death at Nuremberg and hanged them?"[36]

Four years earlier, in 1956, the great Oxford philosopher and Catholic thinker Elizabeth Anscombe had made a still more enlightening comparison. Let us suppose, she said, that the Allies had thought at the beginning of 1945 that, in order to break the Germans' will to resist and to compel them to surrender rapidly and unconditionally, thus sparing the lives of a great many Allied soldiers, it was necessary to carry out the massacre of hundreds of thousands of civilians, women and children included, in two cities in the Ruhr. Two questions arise. First, what difference would there have been, morally speaking, between this and what the Nazis did in Czechoslovakia and Poland? Second, what difference would there have been, morally speaking, between this and the atomic bombing of Hiroshima and Nagasaki?[37]

Moral philosophy is forced to resort to analogies of this sort, in the face of sheer horror, for it has nothing other than logical consistency on which to base the validity of its arguments. In the event, this minimal requirement of consistency did not suffice to rule out the nuclear option. Why? One possible reply is that morality was nothing more than a convenient pretext. A revisionist school of American historians led by Gar Alperovitz has vigorously pleaded this case, arguing that in July 1945 Japan was on the point of capitulation.[38] Two conditions would have been sufficient to obtain immediate surrender: first, that President Truman persuade the Soviet Union to declare war on Japan immediately, rather than wait until 8 August, the date agreed upon at the Yalta Conference in February 1945; second, that Japanese surrender be accompanied by an American promise that the emperor would be allowed to continue to sit on his throne. Truman refused both conditions at the conference at Potsdam, convened on 17 July 1945. The day before, the president had received "good news." The bomb was ready—as the successful test at Alamogordo had brilliantly demonstrated. On his way home from Potsdam, on 7 August, which is to say the day before the signing of the Nuremberg charter, Truman issued this triumphal declaration: "We have spent 2 billion dollars on the greatest scientific gamble in history— and won."[39]

The revisionist interpretation gives rise in its turn to two further questions. First, how are we to make sense of the bombing of Hiroshima—and, more troubling still, of Nagasaki, which is to say the grotesquely absurd determination to persist in infamy? Second, how could the "ethical" veneer of the official justification for these acts—that they were extremely regrettable, but a moral necessity just the same—have been accepted as a lawful defense, when it should have been seen instead as the most execrable and appalling excuse imaginable?

Not only does the work of Günther Anders furnish an answer to these questions, it does so by relocating them in another context. Anders, a German Jew who had emigrated to France and from there to America, and then come back to Europe in 1950—everywhere an exile, always the wandering Jew—recognized that on 6 August 1945 human history had entered into a new phase, its last. Or rather that the sixth day of August was only a rehearsal for the ninth—what he called the "Nagasaki syndrome." The atomic bombing of a civilian population, once it had occurred for the first time, once it had made the unthinkable real, inevitably invited more atrocities, in the same way that an earthquake is inevitably followed by a series of aftershocks.[40] History became obsolete that day, as Anders put it.[41] Now that humanity was capable of destroying itself, nothing could ever cause it to lose this "negative all-powerfulness," not even a general disarmament, not even a total denuclearization of the world's arsenals. Apocalypse having been inscribed in our future as fate, the best we can do is to indefinitely postpone the final moment. We are now living under a suspended sentence, as it were, a stay of execution. In August 1945, Anders said, humanity entered into an era of reprieve (*die Frist*), the "second death" of all that had existed: since the meaning of the past depends on future actions, the obsolescence of the future, its programmed end, signifies not that the past no longer has any meaning, but that it will never have had one.[42] The parable of Noah and the flood with which I began says this admirably well.

To inquire into the rationality and the morality of the destruction of Hiroshima and Nagasaki amounts to treating nuclear weapons as a means in the service of an end. A means loses itself in its end as a river loses itself in the sea, and ends up being completely absorbed by it. But the bomb ended up exceeding all the ends that could ever be given to it, or ever found for it. The question whether the end justifies the means suddenly became obsolete, like everything else. Why was the bomb used? Because it *existed*. The simple fact of its existence is a threat, or rather a promise that it will be used. Why has the moral horror of its use not been perceived? What accounts for this "blindness in the face of apocalypse"? Because beyond certain thresholds, our power of making and doing infinitely exceeds our capacity for feeling and imagining. It is this irreducible gap that Anders called the "Promethean discrepancy."[43]

Arendt diagnosed Eichmann's psychological disability as a "lack of imagination."[44] Anders showed that this is not the weakness of any one person in particular; it is the weakness of every person when mankind's capacity for invention, and for destruction, becomes disproportionately enlarged in relation to the human condition.[45] Major Claude Eatherly, one of the pilots of the bomber fleet that destroyed Hiroshima, was ravaged by guilt for what he had done. Finding it unbearable to be treated as a hero, he took to committing petty crimes in order to ensure that he would be punished, at least, if not also the country he served. The American authorities had Eatherly committed to a psychiatric hospital, arguing that he was mentally defective—someone who, in the eyes of the law, is not responsible for his actions. Anders subsequently entered into a correspondence with this anti-Eichmann, trying to prove to him that, by acting in accordance with the norms of ordinary morality in a situation that exhausted all available moral resources, he showed himself to be of sound mind and fully responsible for his participation in a criminal act of momentous magnitude.[46]

The structural analogy with Auschwitz and most great moral evils is plain. Claude Eatherly could have considered himself a mere cog in the machinery of war. After all, he did no more than report the weather conditions over Hiroshima to Colonel Paul Tibbets, who was flying an hour behind him in the B-29 that carried the "Little Boy" bomb. After giving the green light, Eatherly turned back and never saw the bomb blast or the atomic cloud that rose up from it. Unlike Eichmann, however, he refused to discount his responsibility in relation to what he actually did (or claimed to have actually done). Anders helped him see that, despite his confused state of mind, he had intuited something true and profound, namely, that a great crime may result from a concatenation of small steps taken by a succession of "thoughtless" agents.

I have tried in my own work to broaden the scope of Günther Anders's analysis by extending it to the question of nuclear deterrence.[47] For more than four decades during the Cold War, the situation of reciprocal vulnerability (or "mutual assured destruction") assigned a major role to the notion of *deterrent intention*, on both the strategic and the moral level. "Our submarines will be capable of killing fifty million people in a half-hour," a French nuclear strategist once blithely observed. "We think that this suffices to deter any adversary."[48] The unsurpassably horrifying threat expressed by such a statement is the very essence of deterrence. That an unfathomable abomination should have been considered the height of wisdom, and that it should have been credited with having kept world peace during a period whose relative stability appears to some more desirable than the chaos we are experiencing today, is beyond the pale even of the infernal realm marked out by the memory of Auschwitz and Hiroshima. Few persons were at all troubled by this state of affairs, however, apart from American bishops— and President Reagan. Once again we cannot avoid asking the obvious question: why?

For many years the usual reply was that what is at issue here is an intention, not the carrying out of an intention. What is more, it is an intention of an exceedingly special kind: the very fact of its being formed has the consequence, in principle at least, that the conditions that would lead to its being acted on are not realized. One forms a deterrent intention, in other words, in order not to put it into effect. Specialists speak of such intentions as being inherently "self-stultifying."[49] But this plainly does no more than give a name to an enigma. It does nothing to resolve it.

No one who thinks about the strategic and moral status of deterrent intention can fail to be overwhelmed by paradox. What seems to shield deterrent intention from ethical rebuke is the very thing that renders it useless from a strategic point of view, for the morality of such an intention appears to depend on the existence of a meta-intention . . . not to act on it. Deterrent intention, like primitive divinities, appears to unite absolute goodness, since it is thanks to this intention that nuclear war has not taken place, with absolute evil, since the act it intends is an unutterable infamy.

Eventually it came to be perceived that nuclear deterrence has no need of deterrent intention in order to be effective.[50] The god of intention turned out to be a false idol since, in principle, the mere existence of two deadly arsenals pointed at each other, without the least threat of their use being made or even implied, is enough to keep the warheads locked away in their silos. Even so, the specter of nuclear apocalypse did not disappear from the world; nor did a certain form of transcendence. Under the name "existential" deterrence, the perils of the old regime were transformed in such a way that mutual annihilation now loomed as the *fate* of humanity, its destiny. To say that deterrence worked means simply this: so long as one does not recklessly tempt fate, there is a chance that it will forget us—for a time, perhaps a long, indeed a very long time; but not forever.

To believe the theory of existential deterrence, nuclear weapons have managed to keep the world at peace until now by projecting evil outside the sphere of human experience, by making it an evil without harmful intent; an evil capable of annihilating civilization, though with no more malice than an earthquake or a tsunami; an evil whose destructive force can only make nature herself envious. The threat hanging over the heads of the world's leaders has caused them to exercise the caution necessary to avoid the biblical abomination of desolation promised by thermonuclear war, decimating entire nations and, in the worst case, extinguishing life on earth.

The evil that inhabits the so-called nuclear peace, unmoored from any malign intention, inspires these words of terrifying insight in Anders's book, *Hiroshima Is Everywhere*: "The fantastic character of the situation quite simply takes one's breath away. At the very moment when the world becomes apocalyptic, and this owing to our own fault, it presents the image . . . of a paradise inhabited by murderers without malice and victims without hatred. Nowhere is there any trace of malice, there is only rubble." These words are followed by a spine-chilling prophecy: "No war in history will have been more devoid of hatred than the war by tele-murder that is to come. . . . [T]his absence of hatred will be the most inhuman absence of hatred that has ever existed; absence of hatred and absence of scruples will henceforth be one and the same."[51]

But, above all, it becomes apparent that nuclear deterrence can function effectively and "ethically"—by which I mean, function in a way that allays our qualms of conscience by blinding us to the apocalypse—only by making apocalypse part of a timeless transcendence, like the God of Saint Thomas Aquinas. In this sense, like the flood in Anders's account, the apocalypse *has already taken place*, since the past and future are merged in an eternal present. Hiroshima is always, just as it is everywhere.

◆   ◆   ◆

In 1958, Günther Anders traveled to Hiroshima and Nagasaki to take part in
the Fourth World Conference against Atomic and Hydrogen Bombs. After
many conversations with survivors of the catastrophe, he noted in his diary:
"Their steadfast resolve not to speak of those who were to blame, not to say
that the event had been caused by human beings; not to harbor the least
resentment, even though they were the victims of the greatest of crimes—
this really is too much for me, it passes all understanding." And he added:
"They constantly speak of the catastrophe as if it were an earthquake or a
tidal wave. They use the Japanese word, *tsunami*."[52]

    Having set off from Lisbon toward Hiroshima, have we now inadver-
tently come back to our point of departure?

CHAPTER 4

The Problem of Future Catastrophe

Take heed, be watchful; for you do not know when the time will come.

—Mark 13:33

We are naturally inclined to suppose that there must be a vast difference, morally speaking, between the victims of the Shoah and the bombing of Hiroshima, on the one hand, and those of the tsunami of December 2004, on the other. It is plain from what I have said so far, however, that the distinction between these two classes has been blurred, and that the result of conflating them has often been anger and resentment. In trying to clear up this confusion, it will be helpful to consider another class of victims, probably the first ones of their kind since it is to them that we owe the very word "victim"—sacrificial victims, that is, animals or human beings offered in sacrifice to a divinity. We have therefore three categories to consider, rather than merely two: sacrificial victims, the victims of massacres, and the victims of natural catastrophes.

The Confusion of Victims

On 11 September 2001, New Yorkers—and, in sympathy with them, the vast majority of Americans—spontaneously looked upon the place where the twin towers were struck down by the terrorists that day as a "sacred space." There is no doubt that they did this unreflectively, for on many occasions afterward they asked themselves what had prompted them to take this view. Was it because they saw in the event a manifestation of divine purpose? But surely no god, at least no god recognized by most Americans, would have sanctioned such an abomination. Were they inspired by the martyrdom undergone by the victims in defense of American values ("democracy, pluralism, and productivity," as one Internet discussion group enumerated them), which the terrorists are often said to have hated above all else? But many of the victims were not American, and no doubt at least some of them did not share all of these values, having been chosen, as it were, at random or, rather, blindly. This is a question that I regularly pose to my students in the United States, and I have still to this day not received an answer that they themselves are satisfied with.

We must turn to anthropology for the rudiments of an answer. Hubert and Mauss, in their *Essay on the Nature and Function of Sacrifice* (1898),[1] came up against the following paradox: it is criminal to have killed a victim, because he is sacred; but he cannot be sacred if he has not been killed. "If sacrifice resembles criminal violence," René Girard later observed, "we may say that there is, inversely, hardly any form of violence that cannot be described in terms of sacrifice—as Greek tragedy clearly reveals. . . . [S]acrifice and murder would not lend themselves to this game of reciprocal substitution if they were not in some way related."[2] Accordingly, the answer to the question I posed a moment ago is simply this: what renders the site of the 9/11 terrorist attack sacred is the very violence that was committed there. To call the annihilation of the European Jews a "holocaust" exhibits the same logic, and responds to the same impulse.

It was during his trip to Japan, in 1958, that Günther Anders learned of the appearance of a new book by Karl Jaspers, *The Atomic Bomb and the Future of Man*.[3] Someone told him that Jaspers had written that a "radical 'no' to the atomic bomb includes the willingness to submit to totalitarianism," and warned that "one must not conceal from oneself the possibility of having in the near future to decide between totalitarian domination and the atomic bomb." Anders was outraged above all by the use that Jaspers made of the words "sacrifice," "victim," and "sacrificial victim."[4] In order to prevent any form of totalitarianism from taking over the planet, Jaspers argued, it would be necessary to use the bomb and consent to a "total sacrifice." Anders confided this remark to his diary: "In the worst case, according to Jaspers, it might become morally inevitable . . . to risk the sacrifice of the victim, and therefore of humanity. I want to know *who*, therefore, according to Jaspers, would sacrifice *whom*? And *to whom* would the sacrifice be made?" He went on to say this:

> If only [Jaspers] had contented himself with the sober phrase "suicide of humanity"; that is to say: in the worst case, it might become morally inevitable . . . that humanity kill itself—which would be quite mad enough. For it could not be said that the millions of those who would be annihilated with their children and grandchildren during an atomic war, that these millions meant to collectively commit suicide. They would not sacrifice themselves, they *would be* "sacrificed." The only undeceitful term that would be left [in that case] is "murder." As a consequence: if need be, it might become inevitable to assassinate humanity. Grotesque! I could not believe, until I saw it clearly and with my own eyes, that Jaspers would replace the term "murder" . . . by "sacrificing oneself."[5]

What appalled Anders was the recourse to a religious vocabulary in order to hide an unspeakable abomination. And yet Anders, a committed atheist, himself recognized the existence of a form of transcendence: "What I recognize as being 'religious' in nature is nothing at all positive, but only the horror of human action transcending any human scale, which no God can prevent."[6] What Anders did not grasp was that it is precisely this negative transcendence that legitimizes the terminology of victim and sacrifice. The fundamental disagreement between Anders and Jaspers can be epitomized in the following way: whereas Jaspers regarded the bomb as an instrument in the service of an end, and the victims as the necessary price of preserving liberty, Anders argued, in effect, that the use of the bomb could not be considered a sacrificial act, since the only divinity or transcendence that remains in that case is the bomb itself.

Now, if Anders had read Hubert and Mauss's essay on sacrifice, he would have understood that this confusion between the sacrificer, the victim, and the divinity constitutes the very essence of sacrifice. In Mexico, the two anthropologists observed, "at the festival of the god Totec, prisoners were killed and flayed, and a priest donned the skin of one of them and became the image of the god. He wore the god's ornaments and garb, sat on a throne, and received in his place the images of the first fruits." The sacrifice *to* the god was only a form derived from the sacrifice *of* the god: in the beginning, "It is . . . the god who undergoes the sacrifice." In other words, Hubert and Mauss conclude, "*The god was offered to himself.*"[7]

In matters of religion, the confusion of categories may be a sign of lucidity—whereas clear and distinct ideas are apt to be misleading. We are accustomed to assume that sacrifice involves the offering of a victim to a divinity through the intercession of an agent, the priest or sacrificer. To the extent we no longer believe in the existence of a divinity, however, it seems natural to conclude that the sacrifice corresponds to nothing real.[8] But the account given by Hubert and Mauss enjoins us to conflate what rational analysis distinguishes: not only does the god emanate from the victim, "He must still possess his divine nature in its entirety at the moment when he enters . . . into the sacrifice to become a victim himself."[9] To be sure, the circular form of the logic of sacrifice has the appearance of paradox. But the same conundrum is found at the heart of many philosophical or theoretical systems that like to think of themselves as being perfectly secular. In Rousseau, for example, the form of the social contract is expressed by the formula "Each one, in giving himself to all, gives himself to no one,"[10] where "all"—which is to say the body politic—is constituted only during, and by means of, this act of offering. To paraphrase Hubert and Mauss, one might say that men in a state of nature must already form a body so that they can give themselves to it. If the analogy seems unconvincing, let us turn Rousseau's formula inside out, as Benjamin Constant did so ruthlessly in extracting the terroristic implication of the principle of popular sovereignty, which consists in "offering to the people as a whole the holocaust of the people taken one by one."[11]

The paradox disappears if one follows Girard in regarding the sacred as the externalization of human violence in relation to itself.[12] One has only to substitute "violence" for "divinity" in the formulas of Hubert and Mauss in order to demystify a conception that stands beneath a halo, as it were.

Hypostatized and transfigured, a sacred violence can now be nourished by the "offerings" made to it by ordinary acts of violence. Violence is therefore capable of externalizing itself, of transcending itself in symbolic and institutional forms—the rites, myths, and systems of prohibitions and obligations that both control and incubate violence, containing it in the two senses of the word: they hold violence in check while being at the same time created from it. Anders's negative transcendence corresponds to this schema.

The concept of self-exteriorization is also at the heart of the work of one of the most influential social philosophers of the twentieth century. Friedrich von Hayek, the heir in this regard to the thinkers of the Scottish Enlightenment, held that society is an unplanned, or emergent, consequence of human action, and furthermore that the social order does not stand in a relation of transcendence to individual behaviors, as Durkheim claimed, but of *self-transcendence*; in other words, it appears to be external to these behaviors, even though it arises from their synergistic interaction. Hayek frequently complained that we habitually describe organized systems with reference to only two categories: the natural and the artificial. But the social order as he conceived it is neither natural, as political conservatives suppose, nor artificial, as the intellectual descendants of Descartes and Rousseau (whom Hayek called constructivists, though he might just as well have said social engineers) imagine. Hayek called this third type of order, produced neither by nature nor by *Homo faber*, "spontaneous" or "self-organized."[13]

Violence that has been elevated to the status of the sacred, in Girard's sense, is evidently an order of the third type. What is more, if Girard is right, it is the source of all orders of this type. "The death of the god," as Hubert and Mauss were the first to note, "is often by suicide."[14] If humanity were to succeed in destroying itself, one should have to say, with all due respect to Günther Anders, that this was an eminently sacrificial and religious act. Indeed, it would be the culmination of the entire religious history of humanity.

Corresponding to the three categories of victim—victims of natural catastrophes, victims of massacres, and sacrificial victims—are therefore three orders: nature, violence, and the sacred. I have just noted the close resemblance between the last two. And yet one observes a very strong propensity, on the part of both victims and their executioners, as I have emphasized throughout the present essay, to regard moral evil as a natural phenomenon when it is so extreme that to assign it to its proper order, which is to say violence, seems somehow incongruous. If the figure of a tsunami is so commonly employed in referring to the great moral catastrophes of our time, it is because we refuse to acknowledge their eminently religious dimension.

The Sacralization of the Future

What I have called enlightened doomsaying is a ruse that works to wean humanity from its own violence, by making violence its destiny—a destiny that has neither intention nor purpose, but that threatens to make civilized life on earth extinct. The ruse consists in acting *as if* we will all be its victims, while at the same time keeping in mind that we alone are responsible for what happens to us. This double game, this stratagem, may be our only hope of salvation.

I wholeheartedly concur with Günther Anders that we have irreversibly entered into an era whose ultimate prospect is the self-destruction of the human race. It hardly matters what the instruments of this conflagration turn out to be: one may trust both the ingenuity and the folly of mankind to do everything possible to bring the tragicomedy that has so far been its history to a most untidy end. Specialists in what is known as disaster risk management—economists who devise methods for insuring companies against various kinds of catastrophe—are deaf to any suggestion that environmental pollution, a worsening climate, the exhaustion of fossil fuels, the dangers associated with advanced technologies, growing economic inequalities on a global scale, terrorism, war, and the spread of weapons of mass destruction might combine to bring about this unhappy result. Each problem must, they insist, be treated in isolation from the others, be analyzed on its own terms. So obsessed are they with weighing costs and benefits that they do not feel the ground giving way beneath their feet. One may well wonder whether the rationality of experts whose seriousness is measured by the thickness of their blinders is any different from the thoughtlessness and short-sightedness that Arendt spoke of in connection with Eichmann. The chief risk facing every nation and people today, these experts solemnly maintain, is of being denied a place in the worldwide competition for economic supremacy—as if the future of humanity has now been reduced to something like a Grand Prix motor racing event. It means little or nothing to them that at the finish line a cliff awaits the winner, who will then plunge over it at fantastic speed, headlong into the abyss. For a new categorical imperative has now imposed itself. "In a world in which boundaries are becoming blurred," the automobile executive Carlos Ghosn tells us, "one necessity stands out ever more forcefully, for it is identical everywhere on the planet: performance. It is a universal language. Quality, cost, on-time delivery: it is spoken in the same way in Japan, Europe, and the United States. Performance is a duty."[15] This parody of philosophical discourse is as sickening as it is grotesque. Not for a moment do Ghosn and his fellow titans of international business ask themselves the following question. Each of them wants a larger share of the Chinese and Indian markets than his competitors. That is what is called performance. So be it. But what will happen when every Indian and Chinese family drives on a vast network of highways? The earth's climate system will not withstand the strain. This we know with complete certainty. And yet, though the moral responsibility of these captains of global industry is immense, they are incapable of seeing beyond their nose. Anders was surely right—Hiroshima *is* everywhere; Arendt was surely right—Auschwitz *is* everywhere. As for all those experts who speak of "sustainable development," they do not realize what they are saying. For the very phrase is a contradiction in terms: whoever says "development" means that a certain magnitude grows in virtually exponential fashion; whoever says "sustainable" sets no time limit to such growth. In a finite world this is a pure impossibility.

The mindless race to the edge of the abyss that we are witnessing today exhibits the logical structure of self-transcendence. No matter that each one of us helps to perpetuate the competition on which it feeds, we apprehend it as something wholly external to us and beyond our control, as an imperative that nobody can disobey. It is as though our fate is written down in every detail—and yet we are the ones who have dictated the text of this inscription.

Slogans such as "Choose your own destiny" and "Be the master of your fate" have now taken their place among the many numbing injunctions of modern advertising. We are no longer able to perceive the metaphysical paradox they express. How could we determine the course of the very thing that determines the course of our lives? How could human beings act on a power that lies beyond the reach of human volition? And yet it is just such expressions as these that are most appropriate to our predicament. Like the great moral catastrophes of the twentieth century, the apocalypse that looms before us will be less the result of our malignity, or even of our stupidity, than of our thoughtlessness. If it has the appearance of something fixed and ineluctable, this is not because it is fated to occur; it is because a multitude of decisions of all kinds, the product more of myopia than of malice or selfishness, bring forth a whole that hangs over its parts, as it were, and whose menace is generated by a process of self-exteriorization, or self-transcendence. This evil is neither moral nor natural. It is a third type, which I call systemic evil. Its form is identical with that of the sacred.

Enlightened doomsaying urges us to seize the opportunity presented by our ability to recognize systemic evil. For this evil also has the same form as salvation—if it is not yet too late to save ourselves. Like the Noah imagined by Günther Anders, humanity must find a way to turn the curiosity, spitefulness, and superstition of the earth's inhabitants—which is to say, of humanity itself—to its advantage. It is time, in other words, to abandon the tsunami as a universal metaphor of catastrophe.

The most formidable obstacle to salvation is nevertheless not our tendency to naturalize evil. It is what might be called the Rousseauization of our ways of looking at the world. There have been many superficial readings of Rousseau. I cannot say to which one we owe the familiar view of him as the bard of a lost golden age, and of his philosophy as the paradigm of regressive thought. No doubt it is true that man is "naturally good" in Rousseau. But the state of nature in which such goodness could be observed is unlikely ever to have existed—as Rousseau himself was the first to point out, in the preface to the second *Discourse*.[16] There the state of nature has the status of a transcendental postulate, rather like the frictionless world in Galileo: just as this world disclosed the universal law of gravity, so the state of nature revealed the omnipresence of evil in societies that have not yet reached the stage of the social contract. Rousseau claimed to be a new kind of scientist, responsible for exploring the moral world. In his tireless search for remedies to evils that are exhaustively summarized, and described with an air of complacency that sometimes seems almost suffocating, he was the earliest exponent of what Hayek and others would later call social constructivism. With Rousseau, as I say, theodicy was transformed into anthropodicy, and evil reduced to the status of a problem, amenable to human solution. Neither transcendence nor chance can go beyond society, can get outside it—because there is no outside: society is all there is. The reactions to the tsunami of December 2004 have demonstrated the enduring vitality and appeal of this perspective.

Anyone who believes that humanity can continue to count on science and technology to find the solution to problems created by science and technology, as they have done up until now, does not really believe that the future is real. Because the future is thought to be something that we make ourselves, it is as indeterminate as our free will; and since we invent it, there can be no science of the future. Like theodicy, anthropodicy imagines the future as having a tree-branching structure that generates a catalogue of possible outcomes. The future that comes to pass is the outcome that we will have chosen. But denying that the future is real presents a potentially fatal metaphysical obstacle. For if the future is not real, a future catastrophe is not real either. Confident in our ability to avoid disaster, we do not consider it to be a threat. This is the vicious circle that the method of enlightened doomsaying tries to break.

The terrifying prospects imagined for us by our experts notwithstanding, one observes the most startling impassivity on all sides today, the most imperturbable indifference. I said at the outset that my stomach had been turned by the spectacle of self-interested charity to which the Sumatra earthquake gave rise. This visceral reaction may be interpreted in philosophical terms, insofar as it is a consequence of recognizing the political impotence of goodness. No one has described this curious state of affairs better than Hannah Arendt:

> Goodness obviously harbors a tendency to hide from being seen or heard.
> . . . For it is manifest that the moment a good work becomes known and
> public, it loses its specific character of goodness, of being done for nothing
> but goodness' sake. When goodness appears openly, it is no longer goodness,
> though it may still be useful as organized charity or an act of solidarity.
> Therefore: "Take heed that ye do not your alms before men, to be seen
> of them." Goodness can exist only when it is not perceived, even by its
> author; whoever sees himself performing a good work is no longer good,
> but at best a useful member of society. . . . "Let not thy left hand know what
> the right hand doeth."[17]

In granting that goodness may yet serve a useful purpose, Arendt seems to me overly optimistic. Presented with a choice between aiding the victims of the spectacular tsunami of 2004 and those of the "silent tsunami"[18] that every year, in the form of malaria alone, claims the lives of almost two million children in developing countries, the world extends its compassion—massively, blindly—toward the former while withholding it from the latter.

What are we to say, then, about future catastrophes? How can we hear the cries of distress of the *Ungeborenen*, all those children who have not yet been born?[19] Compassion would not be more clear-sighted in this case than in the case of disasters that we see with our own eyes; what is more, it is impossible. And yet, without feeling, without emotion, how are we to impart enough reality to catastrophe for it to be a part of the future? This is the impasse from which I have tried to find a way out, following Hans Jonas: "The imagined fate of future men, let alone that of the planet, which affects neither me nor anyone else still connected with me by the bonds of love or just of life, does not of itself have this influence upon our soul. And yet it 'ought' to have it—that is, we should allow it this influence."[20] Speaking of this same "emotional aspect of the morally required view of the future," Jonas emphasized that "the *factual* knowledge of futurology [ought to] awaken in us a *feeling* that encourages us to act in a way that satisfies our [moral] responsibility."[21]

Enlightened doomsaying is not a blueprint for political action, nor does it hold out any hope of success. It is a metaphysical ruse, a piece of cunning by means of which the threat of systemic evil can be turned against itself. For want of access to genuine transcendence, the possibility of achieving self-transcendence, even if it is the self-transcendence of evil, allows us to step outside of ourselves and to see our predicament as it really is. This is the sine qua non of our salvation, that without which nothing whatever can be done. The only Archimedean point available to us is the future itself—the thing whose continuing existence we wish to assure. We are the makers of this future: enlightened doomsaying must not be misconstrued as a form of fatalism; and yet it says that we are the makers of the very thing that is inscribed in eternity as our destiny. We do not choose between options. We decide our fate—an expression that, no longer tainted by metaphysical scandal, must now once more be understood to enjoy its full literal force. The future is that which lies beyond us, an external lever that permits us to raise ourselves above ourselves, as it were; that permits us to discover a point of view from which we will be able to survey the history of our species, and perhaps also succeed in giving it meaning. The future is that which we ought to hold sacred: it may be good or bad, without our being able to know which in advance; in either case we are obliged to show toward it the same consideration, the same devotion that a different conception of holiness inspired people in earlier times to show toward their divinities.

Enlightened doomsaying is therefore not a program of any sort. It is not meant, in the manner of Rousseau, to promote what today is called institutional design—since design is no longer limited to furniture and interiors, but now bears also on forms of social organization, even on entire nations that have been ravaged by war. Any project of this kind is doomed in advance to be swept away by the tsunamis of contingency that Voltaire has taught us to beware. Just as persons entering into psychoanalysis, who must prepare to undergo a daunting spiritual challenge that will, if it is successfully met, help them give meaning and coherence to their lives, are strongly advised not to take any rash decisions during the cure that might have long-lasting consequences, so too it would be well if humanity, before deciding on a course of action once it finally grasps, in a fit of panic, the extent of the disaster facing the earth, were to pause and calmly contemplate the wondrous thing that has just happened. For it will then have achieved self-awareness at the very moment when its survival has been cast in doubt. Even for one person alone, resisting panic is often an almost impossible task. Is there the least chance that a world of several billion persons can do such a thing, before it is too late? Only by a miracle could this come to pass—and only on the condition that we do not hope for one.

Japan, 2011

In 1958, the German philosopher Günther Anders traveled to Hiroshima and Nagasaki to take part in the Fourth World Conference against Atomic and Hydrogen Bombs. After many conversations with survivors of the catastrophe, he noted in his diary: "Their steadfast resolve not to speak of those who were to blame, not to say that the event had been caused by human beings; not to harbor the least resentment, even though they were the victims of the greatest of crimes—this really is too much for me, it passes all understanding." And he added: "They constantly speak of the catastrophe as if it were an earthquake or a tidal wave. They use the Japanese word, *tsunami*."

At about the same time as Hannah Arendt, a fellow student at Marburg whom he later married and divorced, Anders succeeded in identifying a new regime of evil. Arendt spoke of Auschwitz, Anders of Hiroshima. Arendt had diagnosed Eichmann's psychological infirmity as a "lack of imagination." Anders showed that this was not the failing of one human being in particular, but a weakness common to all human beings when their capacity for acting, which includes their ability to destroy, becomes disproportionately enlarged in relation to the human condition. In that case evil acquires a power that is independent of the intentions of those who commit it. Both Anders and Arendt probed a scandalous paradox, namely, that immense harm may be caused without the least malevolence; that monstrous guilt may go hand in hand with an utter absence of malice. Our moral categories, they discovered, are powerless to describe and judge evil once it exceeds our powers of comprehension. "A great crime offends nature," Arendt observed, quoting the legal scholar Yosal Rogat, "so that the very earth cries out for vengeance; that evil violates a natural harmony that only retribution can restore." That European Jews should have substituted for "holocaust" the Hebrew word "*shoah*," which signifies a natural catastrophe—in particular, a flood or tidal wave—tells us how strong the temptation to naturalize evil can be when human beings find they are incapable of imagining the very thing they have done or had done to them.

The tragedy that has struck Japan seems suddenly to have stood this image on its head: an actual tidal wave, the most tangible and unmetaphorical wave imaginable, now awakens the nuclear tiger. In this case, of course, the tiger is caged. An electronuclear reactor is not an atomic bomb; indeed, it is in a sense the opposite of one, since it is meant to control a chain reaction that it itself has triggered. In the realm of the imagination, however, a negation affirms what it denies. In reality, the other realm that we inhabit, the tiger escapes from its cage from time to time. And in Japan, more than elsewhere, the military and peaceful uses of nuclear energy cannot help but be linked in the public mind. "The earthquake, tsunami, and the nuclear incident have been the biggest crisis Japan has encountered in the sixty-five years since the end of World War II," the prime minister, Naoto Kan, told the nation. Sixty-five years ago, there were no nuclear reactors. But two atomic bombs had already been used against civilian populations. In uttering the word "nuclear," this, no doubt, is what the prime minister meant his listeners to recall.

It is as though nature rose up before mankind and said to it, from the terrible height of its forty-five-foot surge, "You sought to conceal the evil that lives inside you by likening it to my violence. But my violence is pure, impervious to your conceptions of good and evil. How should I punish you? By taking you at your word when you dare to compare your instruments of death with my immaculate force. By tsunami, then, you shall perish!"

The human and physical destruction in Japan has not come to an end. To a large extent the tragedy is being played out on the stage of symbols and images. Among the places first to be evacuated in the Pacific were the Mariana Islands. The name of one of these, Tinian, should remind us that it was from there, in the early hours of 6 August 1945, that the B-29s took off on their mission to reduce Hiroshima to radioactive ashes, followed three days later by another wave of bombers that was to visit the same devastation on Nagasaki—as if the gigantic tide unleashed by the earthquake last month was sent to wreak vengeance on this speck of land for having given sanctuary to the sacred fire.

The special fascination of the tragedy that continues to unfold in Japan today derives from the fact that it joins together three types of catastrophe that we have long been accustomed to keep separate: natural disaster, industrial and technological disaster, and moral disaster—tsunami, Chernobyl, and Hiroshima, as one might say. This blurring of traditional distinctions, which can now be seen as the outstanding characteristic of our age, is a consequence of two countervailing tendencies that have collided in the Japanese archipelago. One of them, the naturalization of extreme evil that I mentioned in connection with Arendt and Anders, grew up with the horrors of the previous century. The other arose in the wake of the first great tsunami to leave its mark on the history of Western philosophy, the deluge following the earthquake that struck Lisbon on All Saints Day in 1755. Of the various attempts to make sense of an event that astounded the world, Rousseau's reply to Voltaire ultimately prevailed. No, Rousseau said, it is not God who punishes men for their sins; and yes, he insisted, a human, quasi-scientific explanation can be given in the form of a connected series of causes and effects. In *Émile* (1762), Rousseau stated the lesson of the disaster: "Man, look no further for the author of evil: you are he. There is no evil but the evil that you do and that you suffer, and both come from you."

Proof of Rousseau's triumph is to be found in the world's reaction to two of the greatest natural disasters in recent memory: the Asian tsunami of Christmas 2004 and Hurricane Katrina in August of the following year. For it is precisely their status as *natural* catastrophes that was immediately challenged. The *New York Times* reported news of the hurricane under the headline "A Man-Made Disaster." The same thing had already been said about the tsunami, and with good reason: had Thailand's coral reefs and coastal mangroves not been ruthlessly destroyed by urbanization, tourism, aquaculture, and climate change, they would have slowed the advance of the deadly tidal wave and significantly reduced the scope of the disaster. In New Orleans, it turned out that the levees constructed to protect the city had not been properly maintained for many years, and troops of the Louisiana National Guard who might have helped after the storm were unavailable because they had been called up for duty in Iraq. The same people who later questioned the wisdom of building a city on marshland next to the sea now wonder why the Japanese should have thought they could safely develop civilian nuclear power, since geography condemned them to do this in seismic zones vulnerable to massive flooding. The lesson is plain: humanity, and only humanity, is responsible, if not also to blame, for the misfortunes that beset it.

In addition to moral catastrophes and natural catastrophes, there are industrial and technological catastrophes. Here human beings are quite obviously responsible, unlike in the case of natural disaster; but, unlike in the case of moral calamity, it is because they wish to do good that they bring about evil. Ivan Illich gave the name "counterproductivity" to this ironic reversal. Illich foresaw that the greatest threats are now likely to come, not from the wicked, but from those who make it their business to protect the general welfare. Evil intentions are less to be dreaded than the good works of organizations like the International Atomic Energy Agency, whose mission is to promote "peace, health, and prosperity throughout the world." Antinuclear activists who believe they must accuse their adversaries of malevolence and perfidy fail to grasp the true situation facing the world. It is a matter of far graver concern that the managers of the immensely powerful systems and machines that threaten mankind are able and honest people. They cannot understand why anyone would think of attacking them, or blame them for doing anything wrong.

I have reserved for last the most grotesque of these catastrophes, which is economic and financial. The vast global market that dominates nations today is a dumb and craven beast that takes fright at the slightest noise and in this way brings about the very thing that it shrinks from in terror. The monster has already seized Japan in its grip. It knows Japan well. In the late 1980s, Japan's market capitalization accounted for half of the market capitalization of the world's economies. Some feared at the time that the land of the rising sun would soon rule over the entire planet. Yet the monster would not allow it, and two decades passed before its victim could lift its head again. Today it senses that the nuclear industry, perhaps the only industry on earth incapable of recovering from a major catastrophe, has been thrown back on its heels. The monster will not let go.

Notes

Chapter 1. Genesis

1. Quoted in Thierry Simonelli, *Günther Anders: De la désuétude de l'homme* (Paris: Éditions du Jasmin, 2004), 84–85 (the emphasis is mine). Simonelli very closely follows Anders's German text, found in the first chapter of *Endzeit und Zeitenende* (Munich: Beck, 1972), a work that has not yet been translated into either French or English. Anders told the story of the flood elsewhere and in other forms, particularly in *Hiroshima ist überall* (Munich: Beck, 1982).

2. The precautionary principle is recognized by some legal regimes (most notably the law of the European Union) as a statutory requirement that environmental and related forms of legislation must satisfy if they are to be considered binding. It may be formulated as follows: "The absence of certainties, given the current state of scientific and technological knowledge, must not delay the adoption of effective and proportionate preventive measures aimed at forestalling a risk of grave and irreversible damage to the environment at an economically acceptable cost." It was first given effect at the international level by the Montreal Protocol, in 1987, and subsequently by the Rio Declaration and the Kyoto Protocol.

3. More recent estimates are still higher. See the most recent updating of the 2007 Intergovernmental Panel on Climate Change Assessment Report.—Trans.

4. See John Rawls, *A Theory of Justice* (Cambridge, Mass.: Belknap Press of Harvard University Press, 1971), §44, pp. 284–93.

5. One thinks in this connection of a well-known joke told by astronomers. Following a lecture someone in the audience asks, "How long did you say it would be before the sun burned the Earth to a crisp?" On hearing the reply, "Six billion years," the questioner sighs in relief: "Thank God for that, I thought you said six million." The story is repeated by Sir Martin Rees, the astronomer royal of Great Britain (who also occupies Isaac Newton's chair at Cambridge), in *Our Final Hour:*

A Scientist's Warning; How Terror, Error, and Environmental Disaster Threaten Humankind's Future in This Century (New York: Basic Books, 2003), 182.

6. Dante Alighieri, *The Divine Comedy: Inferno*, 10:106–8, trans. Allen Mandelbaum (Berkeley: University of California Press, 1980), 91.

7. I am very grateful to David Chavalarias for bringing this maxim to my attention.

8. Hans Jonas, *The Imperative of Responsibility: In Search of an Ethics for the Technological Age*, trans. Hans Jonas with David Herr (Chicago: University of Chicago Press, 1984), 120.

9. One thinks here of Voltaire's *Zadig* (1747). Philip K. Dick contrived a subtle variation on this theme in his 1956 short story "The Minority Report"; the 2002 film by Steven Spielberg that it inspired falls short of the standard set by Dick's story, unfortunately.

10. Thus, for example, highway and road reports on the radio informing drivers about rush-hour traffic have the obvious but unacknowledged aim of discouraging them from taking the most congested routes.

11. Two very different illustrations of this idea may be given. The first comes from the world of politics. The second round of the presidential election in France in May 1995 pitted two candidates from the right, Jacques Chirac and Édouard Balladur, against one from the left, Lionel Jospin. The country's most respected polling organization had announced the previous January that there could be no doubt Balladur would win. The exact wording of the prophecy deserves to be recalled: "If M. Balladur is elected, on 8 May next, one will be able to say that the presidential election had been decided even before it was held." Because Chirac won, as it turned out, this prediction proved, paradoxically, to be true. But what matters is its logical form, which perfectly expresses the idea that the actualization of an event creates a retrospective necessity: *if* Balladur had been elected, one would have been able to say *after* the event that his election was inevitable.

   The other example is literary, drawn from Henry de Montherlant's *La guerre civile* (1965). Montherlant imagines the following conversation between Pompey and his general Cato about Caesar. Cato: "When Caesar crossed the Rubicon, there was not a town that did not welcome him with open arms. Those who come to him increase [in number] each day. They say: 'Resistance is futile. Caesar is inevitable.'" Pompey: "These are the words of cowards. Once someone stands in his way, Caesar will no longer be inevitable." Cato: "But no one stands in his way." Fate, in other words, is the sum of our individual failures to act.

12. When we speak, for example, of the "wheel of fortune," we recall the Roman goddess Fortuna, who likewise combined the attributes of both destiny (or fate) and chance.

13. See Jean-Pierre Dupuy, *Pour un catastrophisme éclairé: Quand l'impossible est certain* (Paris: Seuil, 2002); an English translation is currently being prepared.

14. Ibid., 216.

15. Originally published, respectively, as *Die Antiquiertheit des Menschen*, 2 vols. (Munich: Beck, 1980), *Wir Eichmannsöhne: Offener Brief an Klaus Eichmann* (Munich: Beck, 1964), and *Hiroshima ist überall* (Munich: Beck, 1982). [All three titles are now available in French editions; none of them has yet been translated into English, however.—Trans.]

16. I gave this address at the Bibliothèque Municipale in Lyon, on 20 January 2005, as part of the conference "Writing Catastrophe in the Eighteenth Century" sponsored by Université Lumière-Lyon-II.

17. Interview with Yves Michaud, "En termes d'attentats, le pire est à venir," *Le Monde*, 29 December 2004 (the emphasis is mine).

18. Luke 15:4. A longer version is found at Matthew 18:12–14.

19. See Susan Neiman, *Evil in Modern Thought: An Alternative History of Philosophy*, reissued with new preface (Princeton, N.J.: Princeton University Press, 2004).

20. From the introduction to a debate sponsored by Association 4D (Dossiers et Débats pour le Développement Durable) in Paris, 27 January 2005 (the emphasis is mine).

21. No more eloquent testimony to this state of affairs can be found than the bestseller coauthored (with Terry Grossman) by Ray Kurzweil, a leading promoter of nanotechnology research and advocate of the doctrine known as "transhumanism," whose title magnificently summarizes its purpose: *Fantastic Voyage: Live Long Enough to Live Forever* (New York: Rodale Press, 2004). The idea is that by staying alive long enough to see the dawn of a new age when "interface technologies" will have linked the living world and machines, we will be able to indefinitely extend our physical and mental capacities and, as a result, to vanquish death. Kurzweil makes no secret of his philosophy, emblazoned on the cover of the book: "I view disease and death at any age as a calamity, as *problems to be overcome*" (my emphasis).

Chapter 2. From Lisbon to Sumatra

1. Arnaud Dubus, "Asie: Survivre après le cataclysme," *Libération*, 30 December 2004.

2. Mohamed Chlieh, a Caltech geophysicist, quoted in *Libération*, 29 December 2004.

3. Valéry Giscard d'Estaing, interviewed on *France Inter*, 3 January 2005.

4. See Paul Tapponnier, "Tsunami: Je savais tout, je ne savais rien," *Le Monde*, 5 January 2005. Tapponnier is director of the Tectonics Laboratory at the Institut du Physique du Globe de Paris (IPGP).

5. Claude Allègre, interviewed on France Culture, 8 January 2005.

6. Interpreted mathematically, the term refers to an "optimal" situation in which a given quantity or magnitude is maximized, if it represents the good, or minimized, if the bad. In this case, the quantity to be minimized is the distance to perfection.

7. David Camroux, senior lecturer in Asian Studies at the Institut d'études politiques in Paris, interviewed in *Libération*, 29 December 2004 (the emphasis is mine).

8. Jean-Jacques Rousseau, *Letter from Rousseau to Voltaire*, August 18, 1756, in Roger D. Masters and Christopher Kelly, eds. and trans., *The Collected Writings of Rousseau*, 13 vols. (Hanover, N.H.: University Press of New England, 1990–2010), 3:109–10 (the emphasis is mine). See my reservations regarding this edition in chapter 3 at note 10.

9. See, for example, Tapponnier, "Tsunami."

10. Voltaire, *Candide, or, Optimism*, trans. Peter Constantine (New York: Random House, 2005), 119.

11. In the familiar English version, utterly mistranslated by Tobias Smollett, "Or, An Inquiry into the Axiom 'Whatever Is, Is Right.'" Smollett's contemporary rendering was subsequently modernized by several hands, and republished in John Morley, ed., *The Works of Voltaire*, 42 vols. (London: E. R. Dumont, 1901), 36:8–19. It is this version that Theo Cuffe reprints in an appendix to his Penguin edition of *Candide*; see also notes 14 and 15.—Trans.

12. Epistle 1 of Pope's *Essay on Man* concludes thus:

All Nature is but Art, unknown to thee;
All Chance, Direction, which thou canst not see;
All Discord, Harmony not understood;
All partial Evil, universal Good:
And, in spite of Pride, in erring Reason's spite,
One truth is clear, "Whatever is, is RIGHT."

Translating "right" by *bien*, as Voltaire did (in collaboration with Jean-François du Bellay), betrays a confusion with the meaning of "good" in the line "All partial Evil, universal Good," which can only be rendered in French as "tout mal partiel [est] *bien* universel." French authors have the greatest difficulty in grasping the distinction conveyed by the contrasting pairs good/evil and right/wrong (a difficulty that is constantly encountered in translating Anglo-American moral philosophy, particularly John Rawls's *A Theory of Justice*). The true sense of "right" in this case is the one found in expressions such as "What's the right thing to do?" or "The right man for the job," where the term has the meaning of *le meilleur* ("best"). What Pope is saying, then, is that *tout ce qui est, est pour le mieux, ainsi que cela doit être* ("everything that is, is for the best, as it must be"). In saying this much, he is obviously a direct descendant of Leibniz in the *Theodicy*. And so when Pangloss, that renowned professor of "metaphysico-theologico-cosmo-idiotology," exclaims in the first chapter of *Candide*, thinking that he is criticizing Pope, "Those who say everything is well are talking nonsense; they should say everything is for the best," he only repeats what Pope said. As a mathematician, Leibniz knew perfectly well that the *extremum* of a function—that is, any point at which the value of a function is largest (a maximum) or smallest (a minimum)—tells us nothing about the value that the function actually assumes at that point. The best may in fact fall far short of achieving the good.

[The quotation from Pangloss is given in my own translation; in rendering the last part of his fourfold competence, however, which in the French ("-*nigologie*") conceals a play on the word for a simpleton or fool (*nigaud*), I follow Peter Constantine's fine Modern Library translation in preference to many others. —Trans.]

13. Rousseau, *Letter from Rousseau to Voltaire*, in *Collected Writings of Rousseau*, 3:109.

14. Voltaire, preface to the poem on the Lisbon disaster, in appendix 2 of *Candide, or Optimism*, ed. and trans. Theo Cuffe (New York: Penguin, 2005), 99. [The preface is translated by Cuffe, the poem itself by Smollett. Cuffe omits a crucial phrase concerning Bayle ("et qu'il se combat lui-même"), restored here.—Trans.]

15. Here, and in the case of the other passages quoted from Voltaire's poem, there is no alternative but to ignore Smollett's version and to translate literally, without regard for rhyme or measure. Smollett's concern to reproduce the formal properties of the French stanzas has caused him in many places to distort Voltaire's meaning, and in one place to commit a fatal error of interpretation. When he has Voltaire say in the seventh line, "I can't conceive that 'what is, ought to be,'" the words placed between scare quotes repeat Pope's phrase in *An Essay on Man* verbatim, without noticing Voltaire's mistranslation of it. Voltaire writes instead: *Je ne conçois pas plus comment tout serait bien*—mistaking Pope's "right" for the idea of goodness. The error has been deliberately reinstated in my rendering. —Trans.

16. David Brooks, "A Time to Mourn," *New York Times*, 1 January 2005. [Again, the translation of the lines from Voltaire's poem that follow is my own.—Trans.]

17. One thinks of Alfred North Whitehead's philosophy in particular. See *Process and Reality: An Essay in Cosmology* (Cambridge: Cambridge University Press, 1929).

18. Tapponnier, "Tsunami."

19. Cited in Nicholas D. Kristof, "Land of Penny Pinchers," *New York Times*, 5 January 2005.

20. This concern was expressed at the time by a *New York Times* editorial, "Raining Money," 4 January 2005.

21. Brooks, "A Time to Mourn."

22. Quoted in Bob Herbert, "Our Planet, and Our Duty," *New York Times*, 31 December 2004.

Chapter 3. The Naturalization of Evil

1. Vladimir Jankélévitch, *Le je-ne-sais-quoi et le presque-rien* (Paris: Presses Universitaires de France, 1957), 212.

2. On the tension in Kant's work between freedom and nature, see Neiman, *Evil in Modern Thought*, 76–81, 107.

3. See ibid., 103–9.

4. Jonas, *Imperative of Responsibility*, 114.

5. On this point I find myself in complete disagreement with Susan Neiman, for example, who regards the form of evil embodied by the events of 11 September as regressive, harkening back to an age long before Auschwitz. See Neiman, *Evil in Modern Thought*, xi–xiii, 283–84.

6. This essay forms the first part of my book *Avions-nous oublié le mal? Penser la politique après le 11 septembre* (Paris: Bayard, 2002).

7. Rousseau sketched this essay in 1755, the same year that the Lisbon earthquake struck and the second *Discourse* appeared. It remained unfinished at his death in 1778.

8. Jean-Jacques Rousseau, *Essay on the Origin of Languages*, chapter 9, in *Collected Writings of Rousseau*, 7:310 (the emphasis is mine).

9. Jean-Jacques Rousseau, *Discourse on the Origin and Foundations of Inequality among Men* (Second Discourse, 1755), note 12, in *Collected Writings of Rousseau*, 3:91–92.

10. Jean-Jacques Rousseau, *Letter to Beaumont* (1763), in *Collected Writings of Rousseau*, 9:28–29. Here and elsewhere I have modified the English translations found in this edition, which not infrequently suffer from grave errors of interpretation.

11. Jean-Jacques Rousseau, *Émile: or, On Education* (1762), book 2, trans. Allan Bloom, in *Collected Writings of Rousseau*, 13:239.

12. Ibid., book 4, 13:443.

13. See Jean-Jacques Rousseau, *Confessions*, in *Collected Writings of Rousseau*, 5:531–32.

14. Michel Serres, *Parasite*, trans. Lawrence R. Schehr (Baltimore: Johns Hopkins University Press, 1982), 118–19. [Schehr's translation slightly modified.—Trans.]

15. See G. W. F. Hegel, *Phenomenology of Spirit*, ed. J. N. Findlay, trans. A. V. Miller (Oxford: Clarendon Press, 1977), ¶¶179–96, pp. 111–19.

16. As the novelist Chantal Thomas points out, "The mob will shout acclaim or hurl insults at anyone, or anything. *The object of their emotion is of no account*" (my emphasis); see *Farewell, My Queen*, trans. Moishe Black (New York: George Braziller, 2003), 66.

17. In the first version of the *Social Contract* (Geneva manuscript, 1.2), Rousseau observes: "The more

we become enemies of our fellow men, the less we can do without them." In *Collected Writings of Rousseau*, 4:76.

18. As André Glucksmann does, for example, in *Discours de la haine* (Paris: Plon, 2004).

19. Jean-Jacques Rousseau, *Rousseau, Judge of Jean-Jacques: Dialogues* (1776), in *Collected Writings of Rousseau*, 1:9 (the emphasis is mine).

20. Thus the customary French translation: "Ils m'ont haï sans raison." The Greek word describing their hatred in John is "δωρεάν," from the verb meaning "to give." In English, both the New King James Version and the Revised Standard Version misleadingly translate it as "without a cause," obscuring the original idea of a free gift requiring no repayment. The sentence itself is literally translated as "They hated me gratuitously," that is, to no purpose, without any reason or justification. As against the standard rendering in English, it would more properly be said of those who hated Jesus that while there were indeed causes for their hatred, there were no reasons that might have justified it.—Trans.

21. Mephistopheles: "Ein Teil von jener Kraft, die stets das Böse will, und stets das Gute schafft" (Part of that Power which would / Do evil constantly and constantly does good). Johann Wolfgang Goethe, *Faust, a Tragedy*, part 1, scene 6, Faust's Study (i), lines 1335–36, trans. David Luke (New York: Oxford University Press, 1987), 42.

22. See Hannah Arendt, *Eichmann in Jerusalem: A Report on the Banality of Evil* (New York: Viking, 1963; revised and enlarged edition, 1965). Hans Jonas, one of Arendt's closest friends, broke with her after the book's publication. Jonas explained his reasons in his memoirs, posthumously published in Germany in 2003 and now available in English; see *Memoirs*, trans. Krishna Winston (Hanover, N.H.: University Press of New England, 2008).

23. Arendt, *Eichmann in Jerusalem*, 277. Yosal Rogat, the source of the lines Arendt quotes, was a professor of law at Stanford who is remembered not only as an authority on the jurisprudence of Oliver Wendell Holmes Jr. but also for his own eloquent essay on the Eichmann case, published in 1961, just after the trial.

24. Ibid., 288 (my emphasis). This "remoteness from reality" is akin to the "discrepancy" of which Günther Anders spoke in connection with Hiroshima; see note 43.

25. Ibid., 289.

26. Ibid., 296.

27. Richard Wolin, *Heidegger's Children: Hannah Arendt, Karl Löwith, Hans Jonas, and Herbert Marcuse* (Princeton, N.J.: Princeton University Press, 2001), 56 (the emphasis is mine). Wolin goes on to say that Arendt's analysis of the Eichmann case is strikingly at odds with her characterization of totalitarianism as "extreme evil" in her earlier work, *The Origins of Totalitarianism* (New York: Harcourt Brace, 1951).

28. Today one is obliged to admit that Arendt did not comprehend the full extent of Eichmann's fanaticism and anti-Semitism. Bettina Stangneth's book *Eichmann before Jerusalem: The Unexamined Life of a Mass Murderer*, trans. Ruth Martin (New York: Knopf, 2014) provides invaluable information about the Nazi executioner. In no way, however, does it diminish either the force or the relevance of Arendt's larger argument about the vast gap that may open up between the immensity of evil and the meanness of the intentions that lead to it. Her thesis, as we shall see, had been formulated in great detail by Günther Anders before she managed to work it out for herself. But the recent controversy over what judgment should be passed, more than fifty years later, with regard to her book *Eichmann in Jerusalem* seems at last to have produced a consensus that, as Christopher R. Browning put it, "Arendt grasped an important concept but

not the right example" ("In the Cauldron," *New York Review of Books*, 16 August 2012). I beg to differ: if one does not mistake the meaning of the words used by Arendt, who thought in German even when she was writing in English—especially the meaning of the word "thoughtlessness" (*Gendankenlosigkeit*)—then it may be said that perhaps no one more perfectly embodied her thesis than Eichmann himself.

In a recent review of Stangneth's book ("SS-Obersturmbannführer [Retired]," *New York Times Book Review*, 7 September 2014), Steven Aschheim, the editor of the Hebrew edition of *Eichmann in Jerusalem*, says this: "Like many Nazi mass murderers, [Eichmann] possessed a puritanical petit-bourgeois sense of family and social propriety, indignantly denying that he indulged in extramarital relations or that he profited personally from his duties, *and yet* he lived quite comfortably with the mass killing of Jews" (my emphasis). Aschheim seems not to realize that this "and yet" is precisely what Arendt meant by "thoughtless." It is this chasm between the smallness of a man, his inability to think, to see things through the eyes of another person, and the horror of which he is capable that, for Arendt, is the greatest outrage of all, for it is in just this way that everything that had previously been thought about the problem of evil was reduced to nothing.

29. Dan Diner, "Hannah Arendt Reconsidered: On the Banal and the Evil of Her Holocaust Narrative," *New German Critique* 71 (Spring–Summer 1997): 187; quoted by Wolin, *Heidegger's Children*, 62.

30. Hannah Arendt, *The Human Condition* (Chicago: University of Chicago Press, 1958), 3 (my emphasis).

31. Quoted in *Libération*, 24 January 2005 (the emphasis is mine). In an essay in *Le Monde*, 19 February 2005, entitled "Pour en finir avec le mot *Shoah*," the poet and linguist Henri Meschonnic, himself a translator of the Bible, went much further than Lanzmann, arguing that the use of "*shoah*" in this context is no less objectionable than that of "holocaust." He corrects Lanzmann on the meaning of the Hebrew word: it is false to say that it *also* refers to a natural catastrophe, for this is the only thing it refers to; moreover, the word has not the least religious connotation. "It is a word," Meschonnic points out, "that in the Bible, where it is encountered thirteen times, designates a devastating storm and the ravages—twice in Job—that it leaves behind. A natural phenomenon, nothing more. There are other words [used] in the Bible to designate a catastrophe caused by human beings. The main thing to be objected to here is the use of a word that designates a phenomenon of nature to speak of a wholly human barbarism." The force of this is to say that two types of abuse must be distinguished in examining the relations between ritual sacrifice, massacre, and natural catastrophe. The first error, associated with the misuse of the word "holocaust," is to reduce the middle one of these three terms to the first; the second error is to reduce the middle term to the last, which is the result of misusing the word "*shoah*."

Among the generations of Germans who came after the one that was responsible for carrying out the massacre, one notes a corresponding awkwardness in their manner of talking about an event that signaled the moral collapse of one of the most eminent cultures of Europe. The historian Joachim Fest, in *Der Untergang: Hitler und das Ende des Dritten Reiches* (Berlin: Alexander Fest Verlag, 2002), inquired into the "extraordinary indifference" shown for so long by German intellectuals toward this decisive fact of their country's history. One reason for it, he found, involves the use of the word "*der Untergang*." (The literal French translation of this term, which was chosen for the title of the German film based on Fest's book, is *la chute* ["downfall"]; a more appropriate rendering would have been *naufrage* ["sinking"—as of a wrecked ship], however, and indeed it is the one preferred by Fest's French translator, though not his American translator.) But other words played a part in creating this sense of indifference as well. "The collapse [*Untergang*] of the Reich was certainly seen as a national catastrophe," Fest says. "But the nation no longer existed as such, and with the passage of time the term 'catastrophe' fell victim to one of those typically German hairsplitting debates. To many, *the term implied 'fate'* [das Schicksal], *and with it a denial of guilt, as though everything that had happened had rained down from a historic thundercloud that suddenly darkened the sky.*" Joachim C. Fest, *Inside Hitler's Bunker: The Last Days of the Third Reich*, trans. Margot Bettauer Dembo (New York: Farrar, Straus and Giroux, 2004), x (the emphasis is mine). [The French version is still more emphatic, saying that what happened was the "historical equivalent of a sudden storm for which no one had been responsible, much less guilty." —Trans.]

32. Claude Lanzmann, "*Hier ist kein Warum*," in Bernard Cuau, ed., *Au sujet de Shoah: Le film de Claude Lanzmann* (Paris: Belin, 1990), 279.

33. This according to the personal testimony of Primo Levi, in *If This Is a Man*, trans. Stuart Woolf (London: Penguin, 1979), 35.

34. It is ironic, or perhaps merely a proof of cynicism, that the B-29 bomber that carried the team of scientists responsible for studying the conditions and effects of the atomic explosion on 6 August 1945 was named *Necessary Evil*.

35. I owe to Claude Habib, a leading authority on Rousseau, the following observation, whose insight is far deeper, I believe, than its anecdotal character would seem to suggest. In Rousseau's *Julie; ou, La Nouvelle Héloïse* (1761), Saint-Preux identifies paradise with Tinian, one of the Mariana Islands in Micronesia. On gaining access to Julie's "Elysium," the secret garden of the young woman he loves, Saint-Preux confides: "It seemed to me I was the first mortal who ever had set foot in this wilderness. Surprised, stunned, transported by a spectacle so unexpected, I remained motionless for a moment, and cried out in spontaneous ecstasy: O Tinian! O Juan Fernandez! Julie, the ends of the earth are at your gate!" (*Julie, or, the New Heloise*, part 4, letter 11, in *Collected Writings of Rousseau*, 6:387.) Now, this is the very same island of Tinian from which on 6 August 1945, at 2:45 in the morning, the B-29 bomber *Enola Gay*, with "Little Boy" loaded in its bomb bay, took off in the direction of Hiroshima, followed four minutes later by *Necessary Evil*, to carry out its sinister mission. It is as though history were winking at us, telling us that it has a meaning—but that it is up to us to decipher this meaning.

36. From an interview with Leo Szilard, "President Truman Did Not Understand," *U.S. News & World Report*, 15 August 1960, 68–71.

37. See G. E. M. Anscombe, "Mr. Truman's Degree," in *Collected Philosophical Papers*, vol. 3, *Ethics, Religion, and Politics* (Minneapolis: University of Minnesota Press, 1981), 62–71. The title of this essay refers to Oxford's awarding of an honorary degree to President Truman in June 1956.

38. See Gar Alperovitz, *The Decision to Use the Atomic Bomb and the Architecture of an American Myth* (New York: Knopf, 1995); also Barton J. Bernstein, "A Postwar Myth: 500,000 U.S. Lives Saved," *Bulletin of the Atomic Scientists* 42 (June–July 1986): 38–40.

39. "Text of Statements by Truman, Stimson on Development of Atomic Bomb," *New York Times*, 7 August 1945, 4; quoted by Szilard, "President Truman Did Not Understand."

40. See the address Anders gave in Frankfurt in 1983 on being awarded the Adorno Prize, "Gegen ein neues und endgültiges Nagasaki" [Against a New and Definitive Nagasaki], reprinted in Elke Schubert, ed., *Günther Anders antwortet: Interviews und Erklärungen* (Berlin: Tiamat, 1987), 169–74.

41. Thus the title of his 1980 work *Die Antiquiertheit des Menschen* [The Obsolescence of Man].

42. See Günther Anders, *Die atomare Drohung: Radikale Überlegungen zum atomaren Zeitalter*

(Munich: Beck, 1981). Lest anyone imagine that Sartre's work inspired these remarks, Sartre himself frankly acknowledged it was Anders who had influenced *his* thinking.

43. See the eight chapters that make up the section titled "On the Bomb and the Causes of Our Blindness in the Face of Apocalypse," in Anders, *Die Antiquiertheit des Menschen*, 1:233–324.

44. Arendt, *Eichmann in Jerusalem*, 287.

45. The link between Anders and Ivan Illich is plain here.

46. This correspondence was published in Günther Anders, *Off limits für das Gewissen* (Reinbek: Rohwalt, 1961), and simultaneously in English, with a postscript by the author for American readers, as *Burning Conscience: The Case of the Hiroshima Pilot, Claude Eatherly, Told in His Letters to Günther Anders* (New York: Monthly Review Press, 1961). Note, too, Anders's open letter to Adolf Eichmann's son, Klaus, which I mentioned earlier, *Wir Eichmannsöhne* (1964), and which brought no reply.

47. Though at the time I did not know that this was what I was doing, as I explained earlier. For a summary of this attempt, see "The Nuclear Menace: A New Sacrament for Humanity," in Jean-Pierre Dupuy, *The Mark of the Sacred*, trans. M. B. DeBevoise (Stanford, Calif.: Stanford University Press, 2013), 175–94.

48. Dominique David, then secretary-general of the Fondation pour les Études de Défense Nationale (FEDN) in Paris, quoted by the *Christian Science Monitor*, 4 June 1986.

49. See Gregory S. Kavka, *Moral Paradoxes of Nuclear Deterrence* (New York: Cambridge University Press, 1987), 20–21.

50. See, for example, Bernard Brodie, *War and Politics* (New York: Macmillan, 1973), 392–432.

51. Günther Anders, "L'homme sur le pont: Journal d'Hiroshima et de Nagasaki," in *Hiroshima est partout*, trans. Ariel Morabia with the assistance of Françoise Cazenave, Denis Trierweiler, and Gabriel Raphaël Veyret (Paris: Seuil, 2008), 171–72, 202.

52. Ibid., 168 (the emphasis is mine). I have deliberately modified both the French translation and the original German.

Chapter 4. The Problem of Future Catastrophe

1. Originally published as "Essai sur la nature et la fonction du sacrifice," *Année sociologique* 2 (1898): 29–138.

2. René Girard, *Violence and the Sacred*, trans. Patrick Gregory (Baltimore: Johns Hopkins University Press, 1977), 1.

3. Karl Jaspers, *Die Atombombe und die Zukunft des Menschen: Politisches Bewusstein in unserer Zeit* (Zurich: Artemis V, 1958); published in English as *The Atom Bomb and the Future of Man*, trans. E. B. Ashton (Chicago: University of Chicago Press, 1961).

4. See the French edition of Jaspers's book, *La bombe atomique et l'avenir de l'homme: Conscience politique de notre temps* (Paris: Buchet-Chastel, 1963), 23, 84, 135, 478.

5. Anders, "L'Homme sur le pont," in *Hiroshima est partout*, 123.

6. Anders, *Die Antiquiertheit des Menschen*; from the French translation by Michèle Colombo of vol. 2, chap. 28, "Désuétude de la méchanceté," published in *Conférence* 9 (1999): 182.

7. Henri Hubert and Marcel Mauss, *Sacrifice: Its Nature and Function*, trans. W. D. Halls (Chicago: University of Chicago Press, 1964), 80, 88, 90 (emphasis added).

8. Thus, for example, Claude Lévi-Strauss described sacrifice as "false," even nonsensical; see *The Savage Mind* (London: Weidenfeld and Nicolson, 1966), 228.

9. Hubert and Mauss, *Sacrifice*, 81.

10. Rousseau, *The Social Contract*, 1.6; see *Collected Writings of Rousseau*, 4:139. [I have preferred a more literal rendering here.—Trans.]

11. Benjamin Constant, "De l'esprit de conquête et de l'usurpation dans leur rapports avec la civilisation européenne," in *Écrits politiques*, ed. Marcel Gauchet (Paris: Gallimard, 1997), 169.

12. See Girard, *Violence and the Sacred*, especially 256–73.

13. See Friedrich A. Hayek, "Economics and Knowledge" (1937) and "The Use of Knowledge in Society" (1945), in *Individualism and Economic Order* (Chicago: University of Chicago Press, 1948), 33–56, 77–91; reprinted with commentary in *The Market and Other Orders*, vol. 15 of the *Collected Works of F. A. Hayek*, ed. Bruce Caldwell (Chicago: University of Chicago Press, 2014), 57–77, 93–104.

14. Hubert and Mauss, *Sacrifice*, 84.

15. Carlos Ghosn, "Dépassons nos frontières," *Le Monde*, 24 March 2005.

16. The state of nature, Rousseau says, is "a state which no longer exists, which perhaps never existed, which probably never will exist, and about which it is nevertheless necessary to have precise Notions in order to judge our present state correctly." Preface to *Discourse on the Origin and Foundations of Inequality among Men*, in *Collected Writings of Rousseau*, 3:13.

17. Arendt, *The Human Condition*, 74.

18. In the phrase of Jeffrey Sachs, director of the UN Millennium Project; see "U.N. Panel Urges Doubling of Aid to Cut Poverty," *New York Times*, 18 January 2005.

19. Poets know the answer to this question; see, for example, the libretto written by Hugo von Hofmannsthal for Richard Strauss's opera *Die Frau ohne Schatten* (The Woman without a Shadow, 1919).

20. Jonas, *The Imperative of Responsibility*, 28. [English version slightly modified: *das Leben*, a fundamental concept in Jonas's work, does not mean "coexistence" here; nor does *die Seele* mean "feeling." These terms should be translated as "life" and "soul," respectively.—Trans.]

21. Jonas, *Pour une éthique du futur*, 101.

Index